# In Black and White

BISHOP W. R LAMBUTH OF M. E. CHURCH
(SOUTH) AND PROFESSOR GILBERT ON THIER
600 MILE TRAMP IN AFRICA.

# In Black and White

## AN INTERPRETATION
### of SOUTHERN LIFE

By

### L. H. HAMMOND
*Author of "The Master-Word"*

With an Introduction by
### JAMES H. DILLARD, M. A., LL. D.,
*President of the Jeanes Foundation Board, Director of
the Slater Fund*

NEW YORK    CHICAGO    TORONTO
Fleming H. Revell Company
LONDON    AND    EDINBURGH

New York: 158 Fifth Avenue
Chicago: 125 North Wabash Ave.
Toronto: 25 Richmond Street, W.
London: 21 Paternoster Square
Edinburgh: 100 Princes Street

*To my mother and my father,*
*both slave-owners in earlier life,*
*whose broad thinking and selfless living*
*first taught me the meaning of human*
*brotherhood,*
*I dedicate this book,*
*with a gratitude deepened by time,*
*and a love undiminished by death.*

# Introduction

THE problem of the South to-day is how to find voices and hearings for her best thoughts and sentiments. Especially is this true in regard to the relationship between the races. Public sentiment rules. It rules the attitude of individuals. It makes and unmakes the laws. It enforces or neglects the laws that are made. Public sentiment is mainly dependent upon the thoughts and sentiments that find expression in the constant utterances of pulpit, press, and political campaigns. On this question of race relationship the pulpit in the South is remarkably silent. The point is not raised whether or not the province of the pulpit is to discuss public and social problems. The fact is that the pulpit in the South is remarkably silent on the race question, even on the side of religion and religious duties. With few exceptions the direct contributions of the Southern clergy in establishing public sentiment on this question have amounted to little, and may almost be left out of count. It is the editor and the politician who, more exclusively in the South than in any other part of the country, influence public sentiment on the race question as well as on other public questions. The men of letters, the educators, the educated business men, have not counted appreciably in moulding public sentiment. I said editors along with politicians, but it is not so much the editorial writers as it is the managers who direct what news shall appear, and regulate the tones and head-lines of what appears. It is these and the politicians who are most responsible for public sentiment. For reasons that run back to the awful mistakes and hardships and outrages of the reconstruction period, the men who deal professionally in politics and public questions, and these include the newspaper men, have taken and still continue to take, not all of them but a large majority, an attitude of hostility and repression towards the Negro race. It is natural that it should be so.

But is it not time for a better note? The Negro is here, and so far as human vision reaches, he is here to stay, and to stay mainly in the South. He is not only here, but he is improving wonderfully in education and in the acquisition of property. There are exceptions. There are in fact large masses of

Negroes who are not improving in their conditions ; but the figures of statistics are beyond contradicting the fact that the race as a whole is making forward strides away from gross illiteracy and dependent poverty. Shall the white people wish it to be so? It seems to me that they should wish it to be so. It seems to me that our material prosperity depends upon the spread of intelligence and thrift among all the people, even the humblest. It seems to me that our public health demands this, because filth and disease extend their evils high and low. And how dare we say that humanity and religion do not demand it? If humanity and religion mean anything, they mean good will to man and the application of the eternal principles of justice and righteousness now and always.

It does not follow that any amount of good will and desire for righteous dealing does away with the fact of race. The Frenchman is not a German, nor the Jew a Gentile, and the difference of the Negro and the white is most of all distinctly marked. The problem of their living and working side by side in the same region is a problem, which no amount of optimism can deny. The problem is a problem which calls for neither a blind and hopeless pessimism nor a weak and watery optimism.  The call is for facing facts, and dealing with them in the light of wise statesmanship and the holy principles of religious faith.  Some advanced spirits would ignore the universal fact of race, and in the highest sense they are right in the sight of law and religion ; but in the practical living of our lives there is no reason to ignore racial any more than other natural distinctions and affinities.  There is a segregation which is perfectly natural and inevitable, and will surely take care of itself.  Negroes as naturally and inevitably flock together as do the whites, and in my opinion their leaders oppose any denial of such natural segregation, and frown on offensive efforts to ignore the fact. Many doubtless question the truth of this attitude of the Negroes, but my experience leads me to the conviction that, however much we may think to the contrary, it is essentially and almost universally true.

For the white people the main point is that, with all recognition of racial feelings, we are bound to acknowledge the common rights of humanity.  We are bound to acknowledge that all men are human, and have human rights and claims to life, liberty, and the pursuit of happiness.  Are we not, we whites of the South, also bound by peculiar claims both of nearness and necessity ? The Negro served us as a slave ; in the providence of God he is now by law among us as a man. For his good, for our own good, is it not well for us to be helping him on to useful manhood ? Grant that in the mass he is low down, can any low class, black or white, lie in the ditch and all of us not suffer ?

It is because Mrs. Hammond's book strikes the good note that it is to be greatly welcomed at this time. I believe that our press and public will welcome it as a sincere, earnest, and able effort to tell the difficult truth. All may not agree with all she says, but that is not so important as to recognize that her book is one of the utterances which are needed at this time, and that she is seeking to help us all, North and South, to think rightly on this problem.

JAMES H. DILLARD.

# Contents

# Illustrations

# I

## IN TERMS OF HUMANITY

THERE is nothing except love itself which so adds to the richness and charm of life as a sense of wide horizons. One breathes in freedom under a wide sky, catching the proper perspective for life, and setting large and small in their true relations. The burdens and hindrances which press so close in a narrow, personal atmosphere drop away, and dwindle to their true size in those far spaces which include all human life. We never understand them till we see them so, set against the background of a world-experience, translated into terms common to all mankind.

We were made to be world-dwellers ; members of our own small circle and section of country, loving and loyal to them all, yet members too of the whole human brotherhood : of our own race intensely ; yet just as vitally, and more broadly, of the great Race of Man.

The best that can be said of an isolated

man, cut off from his wide human relations,
is that he has a capacity for life.   A human
stomach, or liver, or heart, may be cut out of
the body it belongs in, and yet be kept
" alive."   It serves no end of use or beauty,
poor unrelated thing, and is practically dead
in its cold, colourless abiding place.   Yet it
has a latent capacity for living, if only it be
placed again in vital connection with a human organism, and receive life from a working connection with the whole.

So many of us lead cold-storage lives, and
find them, naturally, dull enough.   So many
more are vitally connected with but a fragment of life—our family circle, our neighbourhood or section.   It is as if a heart beat
in a mutilated body, legless or armless, perhaps without sight, or deaf to the far, sweet
voices which call to the freest and happiest
things in life.

We are made far-sighted.   Scientists tell us
that our increasing need of glasses is due to
the fine, near-at-hand work imposed by civilization on eyes planned by nature for far-
sweeping vision, for the wide look which goes
from verge to verge of the high-arching sky.

It is much that we have acquired near
vision ; we would be savages still without it.
Close observation, thought of little things,

the constructive spirit at work upon details
—these, inch by inch, through the ages, have
built the road over which the race has advanced.  Long sacrifice has gone into them,
untold patience and endurance, the endless
drudgery out of which character emerges,
like a winged thing from its cocoon.

But we need not lose the wide look, nor
work at details knowing nothing of their relation to the big world-life of man.  How
could we understand them so, or understand
ourselves?  How should we bear our griefs,
or meet our difficulties, or work in hope and
with joy?  Life is such a dull puzzle to near-
sighted folk; and so many of those whose
lives touch theirs are sealed books to them,
uninteresting because unknown.  And ignorance breeds prejudice as a dunghill breeds
flies.

The commonest prejudice of all, perhaps,
is the near-visioned belief in the superiority
of the people of one's own small corner to all
the rest of the world.  This frank and childish egotism is the hall-mark of the separated
life, whether lived by Anglo-Saxon or Pata-
gonian, Chinaman or American.  We are
the people, and wisdom will die with us !
That is the world-cry of unrelated man ; and
it arrogates a superiority which implies an-

tagonistic criticism of all dwellers without
the small charmed circle of the crier's understanding.

This unsympathetic criticism betrays itself
as ignorance by the very fact of its existence ;
for sympathy cannot fail if only one understands deep enough.   It is the surface view,
always, which breeds antagonism.   If one
could understand to the uttermost one would
inevitably love to the uttermost : one's com-
passions, like God's, would be new every
morning.   It is because it is ordinarily so
apart, cut off from sympathy, that criticism
is so often shorn of renovating force.   Its
only chance for constructive service lies in
being passed through the alembic of a living
sympathy, which alone can transmute the
inorganic matter of criticism into food for
assimilation and growth.

For love, and not intellect, is the vital
force ; and no man is shut out by lack of
knowledge from the widest human life.
Things dim and confusing to the mind are
clearly apprehended by the heart.   If I venture to offer this partial interpretation of the
life of that corner of the world which is home
to me, it is not because of a belief that peculiar powers of any kind have been given
to me, entitling me to speak of my people,

or to them.   It is because I am so truly one
of the mass, living a small life in a small
place, walled in by circumstances, like my
brothers.   For any sharer of the common lot
whose deepest desire is to walk in love
towards all the world will find, with the
years, a way opening into the very heart of
life, and will come upon the reasons for many
of the things which perplex us, for much of
the wrong we bear and the wrong we inflict,
much which hedges us in, much which makes
our brothers of a wider circle misunderstand
and misjudge us.   What is said must be in-
complete, and partly incorrect.   One life may
mirror the race life ; yet the waves of personality inevitably refract the reflected rays.
It is offered only for what it is : an attempt
to translate some fragments of Southern life
into world-terms ; to set our sectional problems in their wide human relations, and so to
see them as they really are.

When one lives on a little hill, all closed in
by mountains, one cannot possibly see " the
lay of the land " ; and most of us begin life
in a place like that.   Some of us climb later
to a mountain top, and live there with wide
views, and heads near the stars.   But the
valleys look deep and dark from up there,

the hills seem small, and the mountains fill
the world.   It is beautiful and splendid, and
true, too: but it is only the half of truth—
that most dangerous of all lies—until the
mountains, too, are set in their wide relations.
When men make them wings like birds, and
fly high enough, they see something bigger
than the mountains, and that is the earth to
which they all belong.   One can love the
mountains after that without any childish
pride in them, or childish scorn of the valleys
and hills.

It is so with the races of men, and with
that great, underlying humanity which binds
them all in one.

Long ago, when I was young, I knew so
many things that aren't so.   I could label all
the deeds of men as fast as I heard about
them ; and what was far more amazing, I
could label the men who did them.   Labelling deeds is really not a very complicated
process.   Even a child, for instance, can dis-
tinguish lies of a fairly simple type.   But to
put the right label on the man behind the lie
—that is a different and most difficult matter.
He may be a man who would die for the
truth, who daily sacrifices for it as he understands it   He may be all hedged in with in-

heritances from which he has no way of escape—an example of "invincible ignorance." He may be just at the beginning of things : so many of us tell lies because we are not out of the kindergarten yet, and life exists for us only in relation to our own exuberant personalities. And he may be—though it isn't likely—a deliberate lover of lies. To label his deed is easy ; but how shall one label him ?

Yet youth has a passion for labels. It is such a fascinating way of displaying one's knowledge to a supposedly admiring world. And the more recently acquired our knowledge is, the more superficial, the more, in our youth, it refreshes our souls to display it, and to criticize the little folk of the family, who are still in those depths of ignorance so recently occupied by ourselves ; and to criticize the old folks, whose knowledge has so fruited into wisdom that we cannot trace its connection with our own brand-new buds at all.

Dispensing information concerning its own shortcomings to a world that lies in darkness is, in fact, one of the natural and unforgettable joys of adolescence. Nobody ought to begrudge it to anybody. It is part of the glamour of youth, and dear, at one stage of life, to every soul alive. As we grow older we should remember, and smile. Poor young things, they beat against the walls of their ignorance so soon !

But one's wisdom must be ripe and garnered for this understanding. It is not to be expected of the younger young folks, whom older adolescence is so very hard upon. Their knowledge has achieved little more than a pair of cotyledons as yet, perhaps, and wisdom waits on the years. But they will be as big as the biggest soon, and know as much, or more : the younger ones " sass back."

That is the way quarrels start in families, as all long-suffering parents know. And I think something very like that has happened between the North and the South—between the big brother and the little one. For races are men writ large, and men are but larger children.

Sometimes we see twins whose individual development indicates a difference of years between the two. One had measles, perhaps, or scarlet fever, " with ulterior consequences," as the doctors say, and it has set him back a long time. His digestion was impaired, and lack of nourishment has stunted his growth. The other boy is full fed and vigorous, glorying in his strength as every boy must, and claiming the earth as his birth-right. He wants to be nice to his little brother, but the child can't live his big-boy life at all; and he's grouchy, too—always getting his feelings hurt. It isn't the big boy's fault he's no bigger; and he's pig-headed and mean, anyway: just see the way he picks on folks that are weaker than he is!

The war was our measles; and we have hardly recovered from the ulterior conse-quences yet. But our Northern twin kept right on growing. He came to adolescence first: and in the last twenty-five years or so he has reached that later period of youth when one begins to look soberly out upon an ever-widening world, and to see a man's work and a man's responsibilities shaping themselves from dreams.

I am sure that when I was a girl of fifteen, and first began to explore the purlieus of some Northern tenements, hardly any of my well-to-do, educated, and entirely respectable and Christian acquaintances cared anything whatever about them. Our rector was a man of visions and dreams, and he stirred his peo-ple to open a mission in what was considered the worst section of the city. I was a mem-ber of its regular working force until my mar-riage, a few years later. But to nobody connected with that mission did it exist for any purpose whatever except to save the souls of the tenement-dwellers out of this world into another one, and, incidentally, to show personal kindness, as occasion offered, to individuals of the district. Nobody dissented from the doctrine that whatever was wrong in the general tenement-house environment was merely the outward and visible sign of the tenement-dwellers' inward and spiritual lack of grace : if all their souls could only be saved there would be nothing left wrong with the tenements. There was no sense of responsibility on landlords, on the health authorities, the employers of labour, or the public at large. There was, in every one I was thrown with, a vigorous personal conscience ; strong personal sympathy for individuals, who were to be got out of the general tenement-house mess if possible ; much personal sacrifice ; and a deep sense of personal obligation to be individually kind, and to save all the souls that were savable. But that was all. There was no glimmering of community consciousness, of community conscience, or of community sin. The North was growing fast, but it was still a many-individualed North. It responded keenly, as growing children will, to those stimuli which pene-

PRESTON STREET COOKING SCHOOL, LOUIS-
VILLE, KY.

26B

trated the area of its awakened consciousness.
It was eager, alert, questioning, learning, im-
measurably more stimulating mentally than
my own beloved South: but it had not yet
reached that stage of growth where a social
conscience is possible.  In the presence of
appalling social wrong there was no response
to stimulus whatever.

For myself, I was in wild revolt: but the
only way out then conceivable to me was for
the poor all to get saved in a hurry, and die
and go to heaven.  God might have known
what He was about when He made slum people: but His reasons passed my understanding.

Just then I came upon some old English
magazines containing Miss Hill's earlier arti-
cles on housing, and God was cleared of the
charges I had brought against Him.  The
evils in the tenements were man-made; and
if enough people would do the loving thing
they could be stopped.  It was all personal
still—work, responsibility, and righted wrong;
but saving souls included the changing of
physical conditions.

But good people were not interested.
Those to whom I talked considered Miss
Hill's ideas visionary.  They did not believe
it possible to redeem slums—only to redeem
some slum-dwellers' souls.  I labelled them

all on the spot, and "stupid" was the nicest
word in the list. The indictment grew longer
and blacker as the years went on. I was
back in the South now—the beautiful, Christian country, where there were no slums, nor
child labourers, nor sweat-shops, nor white
slaves. It never occurred to me that we were
too young and small, industrially, to develop
these things ; or that, like the North, we had
to travel through the country of indifference
to the evils we did have before we could grow
old enough to care.

When Stead wrote "If Christ Came to
Chicago" it was the last straw : respect for
the North was gone. They had money up
there ; they claimed to be Christians ; and
they knew. Yet nothing was done. The
imprecatory Psalms made excellent reading.

And then, out of that vast welter of indifference, the emergence of a social conscience
in the North ! There had been already, here
and there, a point of light—a man or a
woman flinging an isolated life against em-
battled social wrongs. But now began a
gathering of little groups ; here and yonder
one heard a word caught up by other voices
until it rose into a cry : and now the sound of
marching feet, and a thunder which begins
to shake the world !

The North is a glorious big brother : and
as the hatred of newly-realized old wrongs
grows within him, as that which is highest in
him is more and more committing him to the
doctrine and life of brotherhood, it is part of
the law of youth and growth that he should
have scant patience with those who are indifferent to conditions which touch him to the
quick. The one unforgivable thing to him is
that a people should be lacking in social conscience ; the one inexplicable audacity, that
without it they should dare to call themselves
Christians. Our brother of the North is deep
in the labelling stage.

And we Southern folk ? If the big brother's contempt has scorched and burnt us,
have we had no contempt for those who are
younger than we ? We had no smaller child
in the immediate family to outlaw with labels ;
but providence has not been altogether un-
kind. For there is the cook's black baby :
and it is so long since we were babies ourselves we can't be expected to remember that
stage of our growth. Anyway, there is the
baby ; and the labels show up on him beautifully.

The North, of course, thinks it had a social
conscience fifty years ago : but that was a

social conscience about other people's sins—
a delicate variety for early forcing merely, as
I know by my own experience. I once had
a deal more social conscience about Northern
conditions than about those of our Southern
Negroes,[1] though my personal conscience
about the Negroes was in a flourishing state.
Besides, we had a conscience about slavery
ourselves—a true social conscience in the
germ. One of our sorest sore points is our
Northern brother's irritating inability to grasp
this fact, which is matter of common knowledge in the South. Thousands of slave-
owners, like my own parents, thought slavery
wrong, and confidently expected the time,
not far distant, when the states would themselves abolish it. The South did not fight
for slavery. We have seen the day, down
here, when we would have enjoyed putting
that fact into our Northern brother's head
with a pile-driver: and it really does seem,
sometimes, that no lesser agency will ever
get it there.

What the South fought for was its consti-
tutional right to get out of the Union when
it no longer desired to stay in it. We still

[1] The word Negro is printed with a capital throughout this
book in obedience to the rule which requires all race-names to
begin with a capital letter: *e. g.*, Indian, Teuton, Zulu, Maori,
Anglo-Saxon, Filipino, etc., etc.

believe the point was open for debate, though
we have long since ceased to regret that the
" Noes " won it.

As for the Negroes, we were developing a social conscience about them, a healthier growth,
perhaps, though a slower one, than the vicarious conscience of the North.  And because
of that conscience, as well as because of
natural human kindliness, the relations between black and white were in the main
kindly and understanding.  I make no excuse for slavery, nor for the terrible things
allowed by it : but those things were the exception and not the rule.  The conduct of
the Negroes during the war proves that.
They are a patient, gentle folk ; but they are
far from being superhuman.  If the main
product of slave-relations had not been
kindliness the Southern armies would have
disbanded to protect Southern homes.

These kindly relations were not shaken by
Negro freedom.  Nobody held it against the
Negroes that they were free.  And in the
white men's hearts kindness was reinforced
by gratitude for the faithful care the Negroes
had given to the women and children of the
South.  In the ruin of the old order, and the
desperate poverty of the new, readjustment
would have been slow and difficult.  It would

have been, doubtless, many years before the polls would have been open to any considerable number of Negroes. But there were matters more vital than votes ; and the readjustment, if slow, would have progressed normally, in mutual kindliness and patience.

But the North, with its social conscience about home conditions yet in embryo, and its social conscience for other folks, like a clock without a pendulum, working overtime, was bent on growth by cataclysm. If it could only have taken a world-look for a minute it would have seen growth never comes that way ; but being so very busy doing things, it had no time to look. The North was a child as yet, and lived in a world fashioned out of its own thoughts. A child can take blocks of wood and put them into a barn or a castle or a ship : it is as easy as making fiat money. But when the blocks are men the fiat process never works : they will not stay put.

That was our great disaster—ours, and the Negro's and the North's. Children ourselves, how should we know the big, strong, overbearing North was but a child too ? And we had all a child's keen sense of injustice, and keen resentment of it. We thought the North understood as well as we did what it was doing; we even thought the Negro understood. Hate sprang full-armoured in a night. The North called it reconstruction: it was destruction of a very high order. And in all that ruin of our dearest possessions the most precious, the most necessary thing destroyed was the old-time friendship between white and black. It shrivelled in the fires of hate; and from the ashes rose suspicion and injustice, all wrong inflicted and sustained, to curse both races yet.

The shock of those anarchic days is deep in the South's nerves to this day. Much which the North calls by a harsher name is a resurgence of an almost physical hysteria.

When I was a child my nurse put me to bed, and was supposed to sit by me till I went to sleep; but she never did. She was a white woman, by the way, and quite well educated: the older children's black mammy had stayed. She had a sweetheart waiting in the kitchen; and as soon as she tucked me in bed she put out the light, and left me with the assurance that a lion and a tiger were under my bed, both friends of hers; and if I ever dared to get up to call my mother, or told her I was left alone, they would claw me under the bed by my feet and eat me up.

That was fifty years ago.  But to this day, as soon as the light goes out my well-trained nerves try to jump me into bed.  When I am least thinking of it there descends that sudden sense of impending claws.

We are like that about Negro domination. We know it is a foolish fear ; yet we are so ready to start at it, both as regards our political and our social life.  Governor Northen, of Georgia, spoke the truth when he declared that "Social equality is a delusion set up by the demagogue" for his own ends : but demagogue or nurse, children are easily frightened.  And the South really felt the claws once ; and the memory is deep in every nerve.

Beyond this, we have never yet set the Negro in his world-relations, any more than the North has so set us.  We have looked upon our "Negro problem" as a thing apart, our strange, peculiar burden, the like of which the world has never seen ; and our dominating thought about it is that this excrescence on Southern life shall never again threaten the existence of our civilization.

That this should be the main aspect the problems of our poorer classes present to us we owe partly to our memory of claws ; yet largely too to that irresponsible, but inevitable, selfishness of youth, a phenomenon of growth not to be averted or shortened, which sees all life from a purely personal standpoint. We are just beginning, as a people, to touch that period of later adolescence where one glimpses the fact that a standpoint purely personal cannot, in the nature of things, be either kind or just, or true to our own best selves.

But while we are learning to admit this, to ourselves and to others, there are some things our kinsmen of a wider circle should remember. They should not forget that the first effect of sorrow is always isolation. After sorrow is assimilated, become food for expanding life, one may emerge and take one's place again, with no trace of past struggle except in a deeper sympathy with humanity, and a broader understanding of it. But assimilation takes place in the wilderness; and life passes one by at a time like that, an unheeded, alien, far-off force.

For years we lived in that wilderness, with no thought nor care for the wide world-life climbing, expanding, outside. Two things we had beside our sorrow: a struggle for bare existence which absorbed the energy of every fibre; and the pride of a high-spirited people who had been humbled in the dust.

Sorrow, poverty, and pride : can any other three things produce such perfect insulation as these?

How should we have a social conscience ? No nation has ever developed community consciousness while its members were battling for daily bread.  A class possessed of a little leisure must be developed before that can appear, and must bear and rear children educated to a somewhat wider outlook than their fathers' bitter struggle made possible. The South is barely at this initial stage.

We knew the world—the polite world—pretty well before we had the measles.  We were a cultivated folk.  But the world of those days knew no more about a social conscience than it knew about "movies," or automobiles: it hadn't gone that far in the book.  Individuals, it is true, were spending their lives, here and there, in the preparation of a soil where later a social conscience might germinate ; but they were thought of, so far as they were thought of at all, as individual saints or individual cranks.  The housing movement had a few disciples, both in France and in England ; but they were not in the public eye.  And the voice of the socialist was heard in the land only to mark him as a fit subject for the madhouse.  England, foremost of all nations, had entered, half unwittingly, upon her magnificent and long-to-be-continued course of social legislation ; and men like Kingsley and Maurice were calling passionately to that void where a social conscience was soon to be. But these were but the local affairs of a foreign nation, as we and the rest of the world saw them. There was nothing in America to parallel the conditions which had called their protest forth ; and to us, as to the great mass of the privileged everywhere, nearly all of human life was foreign.

It was during the years of our sojourn in the wilderness that the privileged of earth began to discover humanity as a brotherhood, and shot beyond us. But our time of separation is ending. We have learned and achieved much in these years. Our sympathies are broader, our minds more mature, our hearts nearer a full awakening. But we know very little as yet about this new old world to which we have returned. We haven't learned about slums, or a minimum wage, or mending criminals instead of manufacturing them, or the abolition of poverty, or the connection between under-nourishment and the poorhouse. Even our churches are still inclined, many of them, to look askance at social service as an adulteration of the "pure gospel," and to regard the saving of souls out of this world into another one as the full measure of Christian duty. Some of us think if anybody says social service and Negroes in the same breath he must mean "social equality," and reach for a gun at once.

But the time of isolation is past with us. We stand ready to take our place in the world, and the powers of youth and health stir within us. We are ready for life in the open, for world-connections and a world-view.

What will we do with the Negro, our peculiar and heavy burden, our puzzle, almost our despair?

If we will quit thinking about him as peculiar he will cease to be either a puzzle or a despair. Are we the only folk on earth responsible for a "submerged tenth"? Burdens are peculiar in details, fitted to the individual or the race; but in essence they are the same for all mankind, and call for the same courage, the same sympathy, the same patience and hope and strength. National trials and difficulties are like personal sorrows and hardships: when we regard them as peculiar to ourselves they overwhelm us.

Who are we, to walk in an unblazed path, to solve a problem new in the experience of mankind, to bear what man has never borne before? Human nature turns coward at the mere thought of it, and excuses its failure with the plea that it cannot be expected to be stronger or wiser than all the world.

But if the burden is not peculiar? If it is our part of a world-wide task? If everywhere men living under such conditions as do the majority of our Negroes are reacted upon by their environment just as the Negroes are? If we have mistakenly counted our poverty line and our colour line as one? If in every nation long neglect of the poor and the ignorant has piled up just such a weight of weakness, unthrift, unreliability and crime for a clearer-visioned generation to transform? If men in all lands, the best and finest, are spending themselves to solve problems such as ours?

When we see our problem in that light— see it as it is, see it in its wide human relations—we will set ourselves to its solution. We never have been "quitters" in the South. If this be our part of a world-task we will achieve it.

And our part of a world-task we will find it, as soon as we compare our poorest with the poorest of other countries and of all races. Skins differ in colour, heads are shaped differently ; one man's mind runs ahead of his sympathies, perhaps, and another man's mind may creep while his emotional nature runs rampant. But under all outward differences their fundamental humanity is as much the same as is the earth under the mountain and the hill. The same things poison the minds and bodies of white and of black alike ; the same elements nourish both. Honesty, purity, love, self-reliance and self-respect—who dare claim a monopoly of these for themselves ? They are human, not racial, and to be built up in all races by the same processes : else Christ were a dreamer whom it were madness to follow.

We need to take the long look, as well as the wide one. We say—a church paper in the South said it only a few weeks ago—that in a whole long fifty years of freedom the Negro has advanced so little that his condition "is not encouraging." If that be true it is a grave indictment of us white folks : for the Negro has these fifty years accepted the conditions we have furnished for him, and been subject to us in all things. He has lived beside us, done our work. If there were no encouraging signs after our management of

him for fifty years, the difficulty might lie
with the management.

As a matter of fact, the statement was made
without a proper knowledge of facts. Facts
show remarkable progress, and under difficult conditions. But what is fifty years in
the development of a race ?—or two hundred
and fifty, when it starts from savagery ?

If we could go back to the skin-and-club
days of our own puissant ancestors we would
probably find that they made less progress
from savagery in two hundred and fifty years
than the Negroes have done in that time.
Of course they had less outside help : they
had to evolve many of their own forces of advance. But for centuries no one seeing then
could have dreamed of the world-service waiting in the ages ahead for those wild Britains,
who lived like beasts in their lairs. If we
could go back and spend a few months with
our forefathers, two hundred and fifty years
after Roman civilization first touched them,
we would probably be glad enough to get
back to our black folks again : they would
never be quite so black any more.

The truth is, we know nothing about what
Negroes were made for or what they are
capable of, except on the broad general
ground that every human race has human

power of development in some direction.—
When any one says a thing like that old
memories stir instantly in some of us, and we
suspect the argument of carrying the sting of
social equality in its tail.  If we just could
rout that old bogey out of our imaginations,
and turn our minds from claws !  Nobody
can force on anybody associations undesired.
And whatever Negroes may become, they
will certainly not be white folks.   They will be
just themselves ; something that will balance
the white race and the yellow and the red,
and that will render a racial service all its
own.   The higher they rise the more Negro
they will be, the more the tides of their own
race life will fill and satisfy and lift them—
along their own path.  To doubt that they
have, beyond our vision, some world-service
yet to render, something enough worth while
to justify their long suffering and our own,
would be to rule God out of history, and to
put the thinking mind " to permanent intellectual confusion."

I would not appear to overlook the existence of race consciousness and of race
prejudice, nor to blink the fact that the latter
gravely complicates our portion of the world-
problems of the unprivileged.   Yet race

prejudice, though necessarily local in its manifestations, cannot be charged upon the South alone: it is as wide as humanity, and as old as time. It is not confined, in the South, to either race. A thing so wide-spread, so deeply human, so common to all races, should move no man to bitterness, but to patience. And we are not denied the hope that humanity will one day rise above it.

Race consciousness is another matter. In every highly-developed branch of the great human race-stocks there exists a desire for the integrity of that stock, an instinct against amalgamation with any very-distantly-related race. It is true that with the majority of any such people the instinct shows itself chiefly as race-antagonism and race-prejudice; yet it is shared by those who are free from these lower manifestations of it. Despite individual exceptions this law holds good, the world around; and its violation, in the marriage of individuals of widely-different race-stocks, involves disastrous penalties.

An instinct so wide-spread and so deep may be safely credited to some underlying cause in full harmony with the great laws of human development. The instinct for racial integrity, with its corollary of a separate social life, will doubtless persist in a world from which race prejudice has vanished. If one believed in an Ultimate Race which would be a blend of all races—a belief frequently adopted when one first recognizes the real oneness of humanity—one would necessarily regard this desire for racial integrity as but another manifestation of race prejudice, doomed, as such, to pass. But the wider and deeper one's association with life the more clearly seen is the law of differentiation in all development. In the light of this law the ultimate physical oneness of human races becomes as chimerical as the ultimate oneness of all species of trees, or the disappearance of the rich diversity of winged forms of life in favour of an Ultimate Bird.

Life does not develop towards uniformity, but towards richness of variety in a unity of beauty and service. Unless the Race of Man contradicts all known laws of life it will develop in the same way; and whether white, or yellow, or black, they who guard their own racial integrity, in a spirit of brotherhood free from all other-racial scorn, will most truly serve the Race to which all belong. What we white people need to lay aside is not our care for racial separateness, but our prejudice. The black race needs, in aspiring to the fullest possible development, to foster a ˌfuller faith in its own blood, and in the world's need for some service which it, and it alone, can render in richest measure to the great Brotherhood of Man.

## II

## THE BASIS OF ADJUSTMENT

IN a newspaper of a Southern city I read recently a report of the court proceedings of the day before. The first case tried was that of a white man, some thirty years of age, who had violated the white slave law. He had abducted a girl of sixteen from her home, and was using her for immoral gain. The judge, in sentencing him, had dwelt at length on the preciousness of that of which the child had been robbed; but added that he had decided to make the sentence a light one, because the law was new, and not very widely understood. He gave the man one year in prison.

The next case, according to the paper, was that of a Negro boy of twenty. He had stolen eleven dollars and forty-six cents. The evidence was convincing; but the judge said he would give him also a light sentence. His reason was not, as it might have been, that the law against the offense was new. It is just as new as the other one, having been formally promulgated at the same time, on a mountain in the Sinaitic peninsula. But the judge's reason for mercy, he said, was that the evidence clearly showed that the boy had never had any chance in life. His parents had both died in his infancy, and nobody else had wanted him. He had grown up, no one knew how, beaten from pillar to post, uncared for, untaught. So the judge decided on mercy, and gave him three years.

I do not at this time raise the question of the wisdom of time-sentences, in these or in any cases; that will be taken up later. The point is that the value of a child's honour and a mother's happiness, when stolen by a mature white man, was assessed at one year in prison; and the value of eleven dollars and forty-six cents, when stolen by a young Negro waif, was assessed at three years in the same place. The judge is a man who has, I believe, a sincere desire correctly to administer the law in his high office; and law and justice are to him synonymous words. He thinks in terms of law, not in terms of humanity.

Some months ago I was visiting friends when a son of the house, a university student, came in with a story of a morning spent in the city court. Some case was pending in which the students were interested, and a

body of them had been in attendance all the
morning. A number of cases concerning
Negroes had been disposed of before theirs
was called.

" I tell you," he said, summing the morning up, "a 'nigger' stands no show in our
courts."

He was evidently shocked by the fact, and
so was the family. They are people far above
the average in intelligence, in loving-kind-
ness, in culture, in self-sacrificing personal
service to the individual poor, both white and
black. But courts of law were without the
pale of their personal responsibility : their
personal conscience, quick and beautifully responsive in any individual matter, merely
condemned this wrong and laid it aside.
There was no sign of a social consciousness ;
of any sense that if anybody stood no show
in their courts it was a community sin, for
which all members of the community were responsible, and which the community could
change if it would. They did not see that
they had any duty in arousing the community to consciousness of social wrong. If any
individual one of the many Negroes known
to them had been brought before the court
that morning, they would have done just what
I have done in days when I had no more social

conscience about Negroes than they had :
they would have seen him, or his family, beforehand, and asked some good lawyer, a
personal friend probably, to see that the
Negro had justice.  The lawyer, who would
probably not be in the habit of taking such
cases, would do so cheerfully and without
remuneration, partly to oblige a lady, but
largely too for the sake of protecting a Negro
who had become individually known to him,
and who therefore appealed to his personal
conscience.

Cases of both kinds are common all over
the South.  A Negro who gets in jail will
send for " his white folks " first thing, if he is
fortunate enough to have any.  And they
come, man or woman as the case may be,
practically without fail.  And often, when
they come, the Negro gets less than justice in
the courts in the sense that he is let off with
a reprimand or a small fine when the law
would call for something more.  But none of
us are sorry for that, for our penal laws, like
those of most of the rest of the world, are
archaic survivals, and recognize no relation
between cause and effect where crime is concerned.

But the very great majority of Negroes who
come before the courts have no white folks to

send to.   Our criminals, like the criminals of
every country, come chiefly from the economic
class which lives on, or over, the poverty line
—from our " submerged tenth."   Nearly all
those in this economic class in the South are
Negroes—a fact which has resulted in our
confusing the poverty line with the colour
line, and charging Negroes racially with sins
and tendencies which belong, the world over,
to any race living in their economic condition.   But it is just the Negroes who belong
in this economic class, these Negroes who
form our submerged tenth, and who furnish
the most of our criminal supply, whom we
white people do not know, and who conse-
quently have no white folks to send to, to see
that they are protected in the courts.—Oh,
there is the Negro problem, and the solution
of it !   The poorest, the most ignorant, the
ones least able to resist temptation, the folk
unhelped, untaught, who are born in squalor,
who live in ignorance and in want of all
things necessary for useful, innocent, happy
lives—they do not know us, nor we them !
There is no human bond of fellowship between
our full lives and their empty ones ; no making of straight paths for these stumbling feet,
no service of the outcast by those who are
lords of all !

In that one sense the Negro problem is peculiar. Otherwise it is an integral part of the world-problem of strength and weakness dwelling side by side, with the great Law overhead laying upon them both the necessity of working out a state of civilization which shall embody the spirit of human brotherhood, and secure justice and opportunity for all. There is nothing peculiar in that. The call to this duty is world-wide : the obligation we share with all the privileged of · earth. The peculiar thing is that we alone, of all the privileged of Christendom, have no wide-spread sense of obligation to achieve this task. We even, many of us, look on the handful who respond to this world-call by service to our neediest as people half disgraced, who dishonour their high heritage in going where Christ would go, and in doing His will with all He has left on earth to do it—human feet and hands and hearts. That is peculiar.

For we honour the privileged of other places who do this very thing. Any of us would have been proud to know Tolstoi, not just as a writer of books, but as a great man willing to forego greatness, and to give his life to ignorance and squalor and want. We are proud of Miss Jane Addams, formerly of

Chicago, Illinois, but now this long time of the United States of America, North and South.   But a Jane Addams among the Negroes—the slum Negroes, folk of that very economic class for which she spends herself at Hull House ——!  There is no more to be said.

Ah, but there is!  We are only at that border-line of adolescence where a social conscience may stir in the heart's soil, and begin to reach upward to the light.   We will know our slum folk yet.   And that knowledge will be part of the basis of the adjustment which is to come.

A recent incident told me by a friend, one of the chief actors in it, throws light on present Southern conditions at several points.

This friend lives alone with her servants on her old family plantation, a few miles from one of our greatest cities.   Her cook's husband, a trifling Negro and a steady drinker, had hired himself to a near-by farmer for whom the whites of the neighbourhood had scant respect.   The man kept a plantation store where his "hands" could obtain provisions and whiskey as advances on their wages, settling with their employer at the end of the week, or the year.   Until poor

52A

SOUTHERN WHITE TEACHERS, LOUISVILLE, KY.

52B

folk learn coöperative buying, after the English and continental method, these master-owned stores are a necessity in the South, as they are elsewhere; and here, as in Western lumber camps or Eastern mines and mills, monopoly tempts some to extortion. In such cases the Negroes are never out of debt, from year to year, their own fondness for whiskey being often as potent a reason for that fact as the storekeeper's greed. The storekeeper usually furnishes the whiskey which keeps them such unremunerative labourers; but his profit on the whiskey makes up for that.

The farmer in question appears to have been an employer of this type; and the Negro, whose poor wages fully paid for the work he did, was soon deep in debt. He decided to hire 'out somewhere else, and his contract troubled him no whit. He told his second employer of his debt to the first; and the man, according to custom, agreed to stand for it to the creditor by withholding part of the Negro's wages while in his employ, and paying it on the debt. Ordinarily this would have released the Negro, as few people try to get work out of one, contract or no contract, who is unwilling to give it. But the first farmer needed his "hand," and had, apparently, not even a personal conscience, or a rudimentary respect for law. So he kidnapped the Negro on his way to his new employer, gave him a hard beating, and set him to work on his own farm, threatening him, the Negro said, with far worse if he left the place again before the year was out. He even kept him at night until my friend, finding where he was, sent the farmer orders to allow the man to come home every night as soon as his day's work was done.

She is a frail little body, but accustomed to being obeyed; and the farmer did as he was bid. The Negro, however, shirked his work, and once more roused his employer's ire. This time the farmer came to the cabin in my friend's yard one night after she had retired. He brought a rope with him, without expounding his reason therefor, and ordered the Negro to get up and come with him. My friend went out and delivered, as her ultimatum, a demand that the Negro be formally released from his contract on the spot. Her simple fearlessness forced the white man's consent; and she gave him, in return, her personal check for eighty dollars—the amount claimed on the Negro's indebtedness.

The story shows the lengths to which the Southern personal conscience will go in befriending even a trifling Negro; and the fact that everybody settled down in peace as soon as the white man let the black one alone throws light on the state of our social consciousness.  It is true my friend said the white man was practically ostracized by his own race ; but that fact was the aggregate result of the action of many individuals, rather than the action of a community with a sense of community responsibility to uphold law.

The story naturally brings up the question of peonage, which is a logical outcome of our attitude to the Negroes since the destructive days of " reconstruction."

Country Negroes of the better type, hardworking, honest and thrifty, are pretty sure, sooner or later, to own their own farms and be their own masters.  Negro ownership of Southern farm lands increased one hundred and fifty per cent. between 1900 and 1910— clear proof that the race is advancing rapidly, no matter how much that is undesirable may remain for future elimination.  Proof, also, that notwithstanding mob barbarities and much unjust discrimination, Southern whites are better neighbours for black folk than some of our Northern brothers fear.

By this steady promotion of the best Negro tenants and labourers into the class of landowners, those left available for labour on white farms tend constantly to a lower level of character and efficiency. It would be hard to exaggerate the shiftlessness and unreliability of many of them. The farmer who has employed them by the year may find himself deserted at the most critical period, and his year's work little more than a disaster. It is for protection against this danger that a number of men have resorted to the expedient of keeping the labourers forever in their debt, and, by agreement with other farmers, preventing their getting employment elsewhere until that impossible time when their debt shall have been cancelled.

It is a surface remedy, which penetrates the skin of the difficulty only to set up inflammation. The basis of adjustment here necessitates an entire readjustment of thought and action, on the part of the whites, to the country Negro and his needs.

The two great assets of any country are the land and the people ; and the people necessarily include those engaged in the basal industry of agriculture. The land produces increasingly as the people who till it gain in health, in morals, in intelligence, in the freedom and joy of life. It grows barren as they are debased. No man, however in-

telligent himself, can make a free man's crop
with peon labour.    For many years the South
squandered the fertility of her fields.    We
are learning of late years, slowly and pain-
fully, to build up the impoverished soil, and
restore it to its former richness.    But we
have overlooked the other half of the problem—the squandered fertility of labour.
Until we build up the worker the material
on which his work is spent will never yield
its normal return.    The houses of very many
farm labourers are more than enough to sap
their vitality, to destroy ambition and self-
respect, and to foster immorality and disease.
Conditions like these filch from the community its capital of human productiveness.

Added to this is our habitual neglect of
the farm-hand's recreational life—the danger-
place of all people of all races and all ages
whose inward resources are limited, and
whose power of self-control is not highly
developed.

Even a locomotive, a thing all steel and
brass, has to have its periods of cared-for
rest—its recreational life—if it is to live out
in usefulness the normal lifetime of such an
engine : and no man, of any race, will or
can do first-class work if he is regarded as a
machine while at work, and as a nonentity

when his work-hours end. Drunkenness
and immorality are the only resources of
many of our farm-hands when not at work
in the field. Peonage is no cure for debase-
ment like this.

The Negroes need to be built up, like the
soil. In cities and factories we are finding
that it pays, in dollars and cents, to care for
"the [white] human end of the machine."
It will pay in the country, too, and when the
human end is black. Christ's law of brotherhood is universal in its working, or it is no
law at all. A Negro of this class, given a
decent house and let alone in it, would soon
bring it to the level of his former habitation.
But if with the house he were given a friend
—who according to Emerson's fine definition
is "one who makes us do what we can";
if he were helped to start a chicken-yard
of his own on intelligent principles, or a
garden-patch; if the educational methods so
successful at some points in the rural South
were universally applied, relating the children rationally and happily to the land; if
the schoolhouses were secured as social centres for older Negroes, and the better classes
of coloured people were encouraged to co-
operate in the movement; if the white men
of the neighbourhood, farmers, pastors, school-

teachers and doctors, met them there occasionally to lecture on matters of community interest, and also to give them some real outlook in life, some glimpse of the wide relations of their narrow toil ; if the white people would look into their religious life a little and do what so many white people did before the war—superintend their Sunday-schools and teach their Bible classes ; if these simple and entirely possible things were done, the labourer would be built up along with the soil, and peonage would be seen for what it is— the device of selfish ignorance for meeting a situation which is caused by our own neglect of our poor, and is to be controlled only by service in a spirit of brotherhood.

It would not be as easy to do as to read about, of course. There would be discouragement and failures. There always are when a thing is really worth doing. And we must expect, moreover, to pay a heavy premium for our fifty years' neglect of this simple duty to our country poor. The Negroes do not love us as much as they did fifty years ago, nor trust us as they did. No Southern white can turn in sympathy to the service of the poorer Negroes without being often startled, and sometimes sharply hurt, by suspicions and mistrusts which peer at him from hidden places, and sometimes threaten to bar his way. But that is our heritage from our own past, and it only emphasizes the danger of further neglect. It may go against our pride to recognize the fact, but we white people, if we really win our way with the mass of the Negroes, and pay in honour our share of the world-debt of the strong to the weak, must live down much of the record of our last fifty years.

But the lower class of Negroes, whether in city or country, do not present the only, nor, I often think, the most serious aspect of our Negro problem, so called. We have many classes of whites in the South, the lowest of which are little, if any, above the lower Negroes in education or morality. This class is not a large one, but it is widely scattered ; and it is the most unstable element in our civilization. It is the nitrogen of the South, ready at a touch to slip its peaceful combinations, and in the ensuing explosion to rend the social fabric in every direction. It is the storm-centre of our race-prejudices, and generates many a cyclone which cuts a broad swath through much that the South cherishes. I know of no solution for this white side of our " Negro problem " but the one to be applied to the black side also—the gradual

upbuilding of character by training and personal service, and above all by the example
of just living in every relation of life.

But control of a situation need not wait on
the solution of its problems. The existence
of this dangerous white class is no excuse for
the deeds its members are permitted to do ;
it but constitutes our duty and our reproach.
There are a hundred law-abiding Southerners—oh, far, far more !—to every one of these
lawless firebrands ; yet individualistic as we
are, unorganized by a social consciousness,
half a dozen of them can sway the weak, the
excitable, the unformed among us, can fire
the mob spirit, and lay the honour of thousands in the dust.

We have lately had, in one Southern state,
an extreme instance of this kind. A peculiarly atrocious murder had been committed
by five Negroes, two of whom were lynched,
the remaining three being hung by process
of law. Some lawless white men, evidently
too poor themselves to need the Negro's
labour, then undertook to drive all Negroes
from the country. Notice was served on the
white people, in city and country, that dire
and summary punishment would be meted
out to all whites employing Negroes in any
capacity after a certain date. The Negroes

were warned that working for white people meant death, and were ordered to leave the country at once. A friend of mine who lives in the county town, which numbers several thousand inhabitants, told me the Negroes were pitiful to see. They went out in droves, young and old, often in rickety little wagons piled high with household goods; went out, not knowing whither, and leaving gardens behind them, and often homes of their own.

And the white people—the law-abiding majority of the population? They were thoroughly indignant from a personal, but not from a community standpoint. They condemned the outrage publicly, as individuals; and as individuals they each protected those Negroes personally known to them. Men carried pistols to protect their Negro chauffeurs, none of whom were molested as soon as that fact became known. Servants came to the white people's premises to sleep, and brought their relatives with them. It was the Negroes who had no "white folks" who suffered. Finally the matter dropped out of the newspapers. A year later two of the Negroes ventured back to their homes, which were promptly dynamited, though fortunately without loss of life. The two houses, the papers stated, were owned by white men ; and the governor offered five hundred dollars reward for the perpetrators of this latest crime.   They have not yet, however, been apprehended.

The papers of the state, like the whites of the outraged community, were outspoken in condemnation of these barbarous proceedings ; yet there was no community conscience to weld the law-abiding majority of town or state into one strong will, fired with a determination to stop a hideous injustice, or to give the weak the protection of law which was their due, instead of the haphazard personal safeguards afforded by the circumstance of acquaintance with some white person.

It is scarcely a step from deeds like this to the murder, by mob law, of human beings. To a thinking mind there is nothing so sinister in our Southern life as the swift debauching of many of our people through yielding to the mob spirit.   Time was when a Negro was lynched for one crime only ; and the fearful provocation is still adduced, at least as the reason, if not as the excuse, for this savagery among us.   But this lawless element has long since fallen below the point where such offense is necessary to set them baying for some Negro's life like bloodhounds on a trail. The curse of their own sins is upon them, and they drop nearer the beast's level every year.

But we of the law-abiding majority cannot lay on their shoulders our part of a community sin. If they do the deed, we, who could prevent it, permit them. There are, however, signs of a wide awakening. The individual consciences of the South are yearly more deeply stirred by these outrages. The outspoken condemnation of a few men and newspapers, years ago, is the common attitude to-day. And more than that, far more, is the stirring, by more signs than one, of a true community conscience at this most vital point. A few weeks ago the citizens of a town just disgraced by mob violence met in public assembly, confessed openly their sense of community shame, and pledged themselves as a people to see that the law was upheld in their midst henceforth. When the real South, the law-abiding majority, catches the contagion of that social consciousness mobs will be heard of among us no more.

A law has been proposed by some Southern man, whose name I am unable to trace, which would go far towards checking mob violence. It would automatically remove from office any sheriff who failed to protect a prisoner in his charge, and would render him ineligible for reëlection ; and it would make the county liable for damages to the family of the murdered man. It would, in the writer's opinion, be wise to add to these provisions a requirement that the county tax for education be largely increased for a term of years following such a crime.

It was with the deepest thankfulness that I sat in a body of Southern women, gathered in Birmingham last April, when resolutions against lynching were brought in and unanimously passed. The overwhelming majority of Southern women have always repudiated the need of mob-murder for their protection ; but it marks a great advance towards social consciousness when an organization representing over two hundred thousand Southern white women delivers a public protest against it. The occasion was the annual meeting of the Woman's Missionary Council of the M. E. Church, South. The resolutions " deplore the demoralizing influence of mob violence upon communities, and especially upon the youth of both races, who are thereby incited to a contempt of law resulting in moral degeneracy and the overthrow of justice." They state " that, as women engaged in Christian social service for the full redemption of our social order, we do protest, in the name of outraged justice, against the savagery of lynching;" and "call upon lawmakers and enforcers of law, and upon all who value justice and righteousness, to recognize their duty to the law, and to the criminal classes. We appeal to them to arouse public opinion against mob violence, and to enforce the law against those who defy it." The resolutions end by pledging the women "to increasing prayer and effort in behalf of those classes, the very environment of whose lives breeds crime."

Here is one vigorous development of social conscience in the South as regards the Negro. The Sociological Congress showed others. It is as contagious, thank heaven, as tuberculosis itself, once the patient's condition is ripe for it; and when we break out with it, as we presently shall, we shall have a notable case. We never have done things by halves.

But the evil effects of the past are still with us. It is true that the crime of lynching is decreasing among us. It is also true that the number of Negroes lynched in the years made darkest by this wickedness was almost negligible as compared with the total Negro population. Negligible, I mean, not from a

human, but from an arithmetical standpoint;
and somehow, by that curious mental process
of self-exculpation common to all men in the
presence of embarrassing or shameful facts,
many of us who yet abhor mob violence
have unconsciously sought refuge from the
horror in the arithmetical point of view.  " It
is horrible," we say, " wicked, shameful, in-
human; but at least, thank heaven, the crime
is infrequent: the millions of Negroes never
in danger proves that.  As a race they are
safe, and they know it."

But they do not know it; nor would we in
their place.  We have failed to use our imagination at this point.  Every one of our millions of black citizens knows that every time
this fire of death has flamed up from those
depths where savagery still lurks in human
hearts it has burst forth in a fresh place, without warning, dealing individual death, and
sometimes suffering for many not even ac-
cused of crime.  Lynchings do not come in
the same place twice : if they did they could
be avoided.  The volcano bursts forth from
what has been, in the memory of man, but a
peaceful hillside.  It is true the eruption
seldom takes place : the awful thing to the
Negro is that it *may* take place at any time,
anywhere, even upon trivial, or, conceivably,

upon unconscious provocation. That is lynching from the Negroes' point of view, which
would probably be our own in their place.
The possibility of illegal violence, the fear of
it, is an ever-present thing in their lives. It
hangs, a thick fog of distrust, between their
race and ours. Through it they grope, mis-
understanding and misinterpreting many of
our most innocent deeds and ways. Individual
whites they trust; but I think few of them
really trust us as a people. They know that
nearly all of us feel kindly to them, that very
few of us would ever harm them: but they
also realize, taught by frightful experience,
that when the very small lawless white element rises against them they cannot certainly
rely upon protection from the rest of us.

This sense of evil possibly impending, with
the deep distrust engendered by it, colours
all the Negro's relations with us. It makes
him shifty, time-serving. All of personal
good that he plans or desires too often appears to him to be subject to the one impe-
rious necessity of getting along with white
folks—not of deserving or obtaining the respect of the better classes among us, but of
avoiding the anger of individuals of our smallest and most dangerous class. To live in an
atmosphere like that without moral deteriora-

tion requires a strength of character rare in men of every race.

Nor does the administration of criminal law in our courts always tend to lessen this distrust of white people. At each session of the Southern Sociological Congress Southern men high in office among us—judges, professors in our great universities, Y. M. C. A. leaders, and others, have stated that, despite individual exceptions, the trend of our courts is to mete out heavier punishment to black offenders than to white. It is not, they say, that Negroes are illegally sentenced; but that, for similar offenses, the Negro gets one of the heavier sentences permissible under the law, the white man one of the lighter. More than one Southern governor has defended his wholesale use of the pardoning power on the express ground "that the proportion of convictions is greater, and the terms of sentence longer, for Negroes than for whites." One Southern judge, a speaker at the Sociological Congress in Nashville, after stating that the white man too often escapes where the Negro is punished for a like offense, added the warning "that if punishments of the law are not imposed upon all offenders alike it will breed distrust of administration." Yes: and distrust of the

race behind the administration.    It will, and
does.

A Southern bishop told me recently that at
a banquet where several prominent Southerners were present, this judge among them,
some of the guests questioned the accuracy
of his statement in regard to discrimination in
the courts.    " And he just turned on us," said
the bishop, "and gave us chapter and verse.
He told what he had himself seen, in different courts.    And he convinced his audience ;
when he finished nobody had a word to say."

It is not only the Negro's well-being that
is at stake in this matter : it is the civilization
of the South.    Through all the ages, the
country which denies the poorest equal justice is the one foredoomed to fall.    It is
doubtless true that our Southern courts are
no more unjust to the very poor than are the
courts of many other sections of our country,
especially in our great cities.    The poor immigrant without a "next friend " is liable to
fare as badly as the Negro without any
" white folks " ; but that does not lessen our
danger, or our responsibility.    It ought to
draw North and South closer together in the
bonds of a common patriotism and a common
public duty.    It is because our poor are made
conspicuous, and advertised, as it were, by

their difference in colour that we seem to all
the world greater sinners at this point than
themselves.   But while I would offer this suggestion, that others outside may feel more
human sympathy for us while yet condemn-
ing our human sin, I would not have us at
all excuse ourselves on the score that our sin
is common to mankind.   A social conscience,
like a personal one, regards the moral quality of one's own deeds, and not what one's
neighbours do, or fail to do.   If we fail to
achieve justice for the poorest, our doom is
written in the stars : and we are neither
helped nor hindered by other people's shortcomings.

Last of all in this connection, yet in their
practical prevention of good feeling between
the races not least, are the annoyances, dis-
comforts and hardships laid upon the better
class of Negroes by our failure to see under
their black skins a humanity as dear to justice and to God as our own.   There are many
points for illustration ; but one will suffice
here—the matter of " Jim Crow " cars.

We who believe that the races should be
kept racially, and therefore socially, distinct
cannot advocate their mingling in the enforced intimacy of Pullman cars.   It is enough
for us to put up with ourselves under such

conditions—and sometimes almost too much. But that does not at all excuse the travelling conditions which are forced upon Negroes of education and refinement, (I use the word advisedly), throughout the South.   They pay for a straight railroad ticket exactly what we pay, and we force them to habitually accept in return accommodations we would despise one of our own people for putting up with. —And we say the Negroes are dirty !   Miraculously, some of them are not, notwithstanding all the provision we make for confirming them in that condition.

Last year a young Negro girl came to the school of which my husband is the president —a school, by the way, founded, maintained and officered by Southern whites ; and after she had been there some time she confided to one of her white teachers the fact that when she came to the city she had ridden in " the white folks' car."

"Were you with white people?" she was asked.

No, she was not.   She had paid her full fare, as usual, and had taken her place in the " Jim Crow " car, filthy with tobacco juice and incrusted dirt, foul with smoke both new and old, and containing a number of Negro men of the baser sort—the kind of car, in short, in which Negro women and girls, and clean, educated, well-to-do Negro men are so frequently expected to travel. There were no women that day, and only these rough men ; and they began to molest the girl almost at once. Shrinking back in her seat in terror, she felt a sudden hope as the white brakeman came through the car : but he passed through, as unheeding as though dogs were squabbling over a bone. She stood it a few minutes longer, and then dashed frantically into the next car, the white day coach, dropped into the last seat, and burst into tears. Thus the conductor found her. On hearing her story he told her to stay where she was ; that if any of the white people in the car objected he would explain her presence, and they would be willing for her to stay. No one objected, however, and she rode to her destination in peace.

Not all conductors are so humane. And it is practically impossible, as may be seen at a glance, for one white man, often a mere boy, to keep order among a car-full of Negroes like that, roused to evil by the presence of a girl evidently above their own social class. A white boy-conductor would be risking his life in such a case ; and even if he saved it, if he started any " race row "

on a railroad train by defending one Negro
from another he would lose his job. So
most of them harden their hearts and turn
their eyes the other way—a performance for
which I, for one, am slow to blame them.
We have no right, as a people, habitually to
permit impossible situations, and then to
throw the responsibility for them on one
man's, or one boy's, shoulders.

Last Christmas a coloured kindergartner,
employed by some Southern white women
in settlement work among her own people,
went home for the holidays. There are
several day trains, but some important home
happening made her presence there necessary
the morning after her work closed at the
settlement; so she took the night train, a
thing she had never done before. The young
woman is a college graduate, refined in
speech and manner, modest and sensible in
her relations with people of both races, and
a strong and wholesome force in the lives of
the poorer Negroes among whom she works.
She took the Jim Crow car, of course, expect-
ing to sit up all night, but with no idea of
the experiences before her. The car was full
of half-drunken Negro men off to enjoy one
of the very few pleasures open to Negroes in
the South—a regular old Christmas spree.

There were one or two other women in the car, and they huddled together and endured the night in frightened silence. The train men, passing through, took no notice of the insults, or oaths, or vile talk.

When she told the white women who had employed her about it, ten days later, she trembled as she spoke.

" I had never seen Negroes like that in my life," she said. " I knew there were such men ; but my mother had spent her life keeping me away from them.—Why can't the white people see it ? " she burst out passionately. " Will they think forever that we are all like that ? Why can't they let us be decent when we want to be ? "

While my husband was Secretary of Education of the Southern Methodist Church, part of his work was to lay the matter of Negro education on the conscience of his denomination. One of the teachers at our one school for Negroes was a coloured man of unusual gifts and character, an honour graduate of a Northern university, and a man high in the respect and friendship of Southern whites in many states. To bring " the Negro question " closer home to our people the Methodist Board of Education paid this man's salary and travelling expenses ; and for four years the white man and the black one travelled the rounds of our annual conferences, presenting the cause of the Negro to our white preachers and lay-men, and finding, as time went on, much prejudice giving way to sympathy.

The conference meetings are nearly all crowded into three months, several being held each week. When a secretary attends them his days are given to the conferences, his nights to travel ; and it is a time of phys-ical strain, even with all the comforts of modern travel. My husband, strong as he is, came home tired out at the end of each annual round.

" How Gilbert stands it, physically or re-ligiously, I cannot see," he said. " He goes half the time without lying down to sleep. If I were not with him, to dash into some white restaurant and buy him a cup of coffee and something to eat, he would often go hungry. And I have never once heard him complain, or seen his Christian composure ruffled. He is doing us white people a great service, freeing us from some of our worst prejudices : and we require him to do it at this cost ! "

I know a Negro woman, the wife of a doc-tor, whom white doctors of the city tell me they respect both as a man and as a physician. He has a large charity practice, but a large paying one also. He is a man of considerable means, and owns an automobile. His home is thoroughly comfortable; and his wife is as amply provided for as the wife of a white man in similar circumstances would be. She is a refined, sensible, good woman, whose influence among her own people is of the best.

She told me not long ago that she went on a visit which necessitated a day in the usual Jim Crow car. I had asked her about the matter or she would not have mentioned it. We do not suspect the reserves of pride in Negroes of this class; and I count it a chief proof that my life among them is not a failure that they will speak to me frankly, as to a friend.

There had been no insult or terror in her case; simply filth, tobacco juice and smoke, coarse talk among other Negroes, and blinding, choking dust. When she reached her destination, she said, no one could have told the colour or texture of her dress or hat.

Somehow the hat gripped my sympathies. Women do so cherish their hats! I am never happy myself until the porter brings me a bag, and my head-gear is safe beyond reach of dust, with a hat-pin thrust through the gathered opening of the bag into the back of the opposite seat, to keep its precious contents from being waggled about.  I can wash my hair ; but a soot-filled hat is irretrievable ; it can never look impeccable again.

Why should this other woman, who loves cleanliness as much as I do, and who is quite as willing to pay for it, be forced to travel in that disgusting filth ?  I know if I were forced to do it my husband and my children and all my friends would feel outraged about it, and would never have any use for the people who made me do it.  Why should these people feel differently ?  It is nearly always the smaller matters of life which make its bitterness or its sweetness for us white people.  We can bear great things greatly, often ; but our courage and kindness and sympathies fail before the annoyances of life.  Shall we expect more of Negroes than of ourselves ?

A Southern state, a few years ago, required the railroads to provide equal accommodations for whites and Negroes in that state. They replied by a threat to take off all Pullmans for white people, as they could only be operated at a loss for Negroes : and the matter was dropped.

CHRISTMAS CELEBRATION, BETHLEHEM HOUSE, NASHVILLE.

But day-coach accommodations are rarely equal. Even where the cars were originally alike, the habitual neglect of those in use for Negroes soon reduces them to a condition revolting to people of cleanly habits. The fact that many Negroes are unclean in their habits is no excuse for the condition of the cars. When white people are unclean, as they often are, the railroad is not excused from keeping the cars in a fairly decent condition, at worst. They may have to spend a little more for soap and water ; but they must take their chances on that when they sell tickets.

The Jim Crow cars come under no one general description. I have occasionally seen a car for Negroes as clean as any day coach for whites. Similarly, I have known personally of Negroes riding through Southern states all day and all night in a Pullman section, their presence known to all the white passengers, none of whom voiced any objection to them. But neither occurrence is the rule.

Sometimes there is a clean day coach for Negroes, and also a separate place for Negro men to smoke—usually a cut-off end of the smoking-car for whites. This is the best accommodation on the best roads. Sometimes this half of a smoking car, with its single toilet, is the only part of the train open to Negroes at all.   Sometimes there is no place for Negroes except in the car with white smokers, though this again is unusual.   The average conditions, undoubtedly, are far below those provided for white passengers paying the same price : and the spirit manifested by this treatment of Negroes is one people of any race or any class have the right to resent.

If whole Pullman cars cannot be profitably provided, one end of a first class day coach could be fitted up as a Pullman, and put in charge of the men on the white people's Pullman ; and the other part of the car could give the Negroes what they now so often lack—day-coach accommodations equal to those for whites.

I believe the railroad people themselves have little idea of the number of Negroes who could and would pay for first-class accommodations.   We know little about the educated, prosperous members of the race. As fast as they enter this class they withdraw into a world of their own—a world which lies all about us white folks, yet of whose existence we are scarcely aware.   It is largely the inefficients, the failures, or the immature and untrained who remain with us.   As they rise out of this class they disappear from our view. There are more prosperous Negroes who would pay for Pullmans than we imagine.

But if the railroads claim that they really cannot provide decent day coaches and comfortable sleeping accommodations for Negroes, a commission should be appointed to look into the matter : and if their contention proved just, fares for everybody should be raised by law to a point which would allow the roads to maintain standards of comfort and decency for all their passengers. We cannot afford, as a people, to let the Negroes pay for our cheap fares : for that is just what it amounts to when the railroad takes the same amount of money from both of us, and gives us better accommodations than it can afford to give them. We are not paying for all we get in our day coaches, evidently ; and if the Negro isn't footing the bill for the deficit, who is ? As for the Pullman company, if half the published tales of its dividends be true, it could furnish cars for Negroes and pay its employees a living wage, and yet be in no danger of bankruptcy. Public utilities should be subject to public control.

It should be pointed out that not one of the Negroes whose cases I have cited, nor

any Negro I ever spoke to on the subject,
had any desire to share cars with white people. They have their pride, too; and they
are not going where they are not wanted.
They want safety, cleanliness, and comfort,
not white company; and they are willing
and ready to pay for them.

There is another grave injustice, wholly
different from any I have touched upon,
which I believe has had a profound effect for
evil upon a large class of Negroes; yet
scarcely any one, white or black, thinks of it
as injustice at all. We Southern white
women are greater offenders in the matter
than the men; and I myself must plead
guilty to the common charge. Yet I scarcely
see how a woman very far from strong could
sometimes do differently; and if one be excused on the score of illness, it looks ugly to
call her neighbour lazy for the same offense.
We demand too little in the way of honest
work of the Negroes in our employ. Shirk-
ing, untidy habits, petty, and often serious,
pilferings—we wink at all of them, and continue to pay honest money for dishonest
work. We do not like to discharge Negroes.
It grates on our pride to be talked about by
a "darkey": and talk about us they certainly

will, frequently with scant respect for truth. And as to discharging them, where will we get a better one, we ask; they are all alike. And you can't possibly do the work yourself; yet if you make them mad they may keep you out of a cook for weeks. And besides, "darkies" are "darkies": white people always have put up with them, and always will.—So we mourn in secret over the departed flour, and sigh for the lard that used to be in the bucket, and tell Jane or Lucinda how nice her cake was last night, and give her the cold biscuit to take home to her grandmother, and a few cookies for the children. And when Eliza Ann brings in the wash with three of the best towels gone, and half the handkerchiefs, and tells us blandly that she know she done brung back ev'y las' thing she took out, 'cause she hung 'em on her own line an' dey ain't been nobody near 'em but her an' de chillun, we falter meekly that it doesn't matter, and that the tablecloths look nice; and we give her a pair of stockings with just one tiny hole in them, and the dress she has scorched in two in the back breadth to make over for little Susan; and we pay her the full week's wages.

In our hearts we feel that we are "quality," and so cannot afford to hold Negroes to a strict account. For fifty years we have trained those of them with whom we have come in contact to rate both our friendship and our gentility in exact proportion to what we put up with from them, and what we give them without expectation of return. They think none the less of Northern people who require a return in well-done work for money received ; but Southerners are " our white folks," and such exactions from them arouse instant distrust in the average Negro's breast, the least of his suspicions being that his employer has no connection with the " quality."

A year or two ago I had a bright little coloured girl about sixteen years old as extra help while company was in the house. I never have locked things up. I would rather have a dishonest servant steal from me than hurt an honest one's feelings : so I take my chances. But things did so vanish out of the pantry ! Cake and fruit just melted into air. The cook was as honest as I was ; and my little housemaid was getting fat. Finally, when a basket of high-priced peaches lost two-thirds of its contents before appearing in the house at all, I knew, like Brer Rabbit, that something had to be done. I talked to the child seriously about honesty as an asset of character. She turned on me with round-eyed wonder, and with what I still believe to have been genuine scorn.

" Well, if ever I had white folks talk to me like that ! " she exclaimed.  " *Honest !* I been honest all my life !   I ain't never worked anywhere since I was born "—she had been at it, by spells, ever since she was ten— " where white folks grudge me what I et before.   Ef it belongs to my white folks hit belongs to me, an' I takes it.   I ain't goin' to work for no other kind."   And she put on her hat and went home : I was beneath her services.

I felt ashamed.   I had put up with her pilferings a long time before I spoke ; and I and others like me had been training her, and tens of thousands more, to shiftlessness and dishonesty ever since they were born.   The wonder is not that so many of them are worthless, but that there are so many honest, painstaking, trustworthy ones among them. They have attained to honesty with little help from us.

I once praised a cook of mine for her exquisite cleanliness, and the economy with which she evolved the most delicious dishes. She really was a jewel of a cook.   She laughed amusedly when I spoke.

"I worked up North twelve years, an' I

learned things," she said. "If I was dirty, or wasted, I lost my place. And I'd have lost it in a minute if I'd taken things. Yankee women don't put up with nothin'; they fire you an' do the work themselves."

She turned on me suddenly.

"It's you white people's fault we coloured people are so triflin'!" she burst out. "You-all scold us, but you put up with us. We don't need to do any better, because we get along just as well as if we did honest work. You-all say 'Oh, what can you expect of darkies?' But we can be honest, and up there they make us. I wasn't no manner of account till I went North. An' if the Yankees had some of these other servants 'round yere they'd learn 'em somethin'. We can do better—if we must!"

Now in all these matters, great and small, and in dozens more which may not here be touched upon, what basis for living does white example furnish? Outside of personal and often unreasoning kindness, where we are prone to take the attitude of feudal lords who give *largesse*, what is there in our treatment of the Negro to inspire him with respect for justice and the law? If we will lay aside our preconceived notions for a little, and go

over all the complex web of racial relations
in the South as they might appear to a gen-
tleman from Mars, for instance, newly landed
on the earth, what is there, outcome of the
fifty years, commensurate with the obligation
of a strong people to a weak one? What
have we done to bind them to us? What to
lift them up? What foundation have we as
a people laid for dwelling with them in honour
and mutual good will?

I do not mean to imply that no basis of
justice exists : if it did not, our civilization
would be falling of its own weight. It does
exist between many individual lives, both
white and black. But as a people for a people the foundation is yet to be sought : and
other foundation than justice there is none.

There is no sense in mincing matters. We
are no longer children. It is the first step
that costs, always ; but the first step is very
plain. It is to put away childish things—
unreasoning prejudice and unreasoning pride
—and to look truth squarely in the face, as
men and women who love it at all costs.
There is no truth in a detached view of the
Negro, or of any human being. Everybody
on earth is human first and racial afterwards.
We must see in the Negro first of all, deeper
than all, higher than all, a man, made in the

image of God as truly as we ourselves. If in the race that image be less developed than in our own, in some individuals of the race it is certainly more highly developed than in some individuals of ours. And whatever grows is growable.

The only basis of living between man and man, whether low or high, which is safe for either is justice. And where there is less than justice, the danger is ever greater for the oppressor than for the oppressed. If white civilization is to endure, in the South or anywhere else, it must strike deep roots into the soil of our common humanity, and reach down to that bed-rock of justice which makes the framework of the world.

And one thing more is needed. For justice is a hard, cold thing; stable and strong; yet must it be softened to nourish a people's growth, and pass through the alembic of life itself before it can mount to light and warmth, and flutter brave banners in the sunshine, for the joy and refreshment of mankind.

There are some elements of the inorganic world so diverse that they can never join hands for useful work except in the presence of another element which, in some way beyond our knowledge as yet, removes the unseen barriers, and allows the two to meet.

We call it catalytic action, by way of labelling our ignorance ; and that which allows the unrelated fragments to exert their latent power for common service is a catalyser.

We are not left without a catalyser in our diverse human life. In an atmosphere of sympathy, of human brotherhood, of care for all for whom Christ died, the races of men— all races—may come together, for service of that great Race which climbs upward to the light.

My only fear for white supremacy is that we should prove unworthy of it. If we fail there, we shall pass. Supremacy is for service. It is suicide to thrust other races back from the good which we hold in trust for humanity. For him who would be greatest the price is still that he shall be servant of all.

# III

## HOUSES AND HOMES

LONG ago, when I was a child, a grown-up cousin took me driving one afternoon behind a pair of his thoroughbreds. As we swept over the long shell road through autumn sunshine, with the pine trees singing overhead and the wind whitening the waves in the harbour beyond, I came on one of those experiences known to us all, when something long familiar yet never noticed stands suddenly forth, challenging eye and soul in a manner never to be forgotten.

Beside the road was a one-roomed Negro cabin, built of logs and chinked with mud. Its one door swung wide, and showed the rotted floor within. At the side was an unglazed opening like an eyeless socket, through which I glimpsed a tumbled bed and a broken cook-stove. A woman stood by the door, a little child beside her. Their rags were thick with dirt. The child looked at us with the wonder and interest of life yet in his young eyes; but the woman's black face was expressionless, her murky eyes unquestioning, unexpectant. She saw us because we crossed her field of vision, just as an animal might see a passing bird.

The day was glorious, our swift flight intoxicating; the swaying pines called to the blood, and the sea sang of wonders yet to be; but the stolid woman and her eyeless home blotted out everything else. I had looked at the like a thousand times; but somehow that day, in my riot of physical and mental exaltation, I had eyes to see; and the shock of it made me gasp.

"Why must they live like that?" I demanded. "Why do I have everything, and they nothing?"

My elderly cousin laughed a little, and then, realizing my excitement, spoke soberly.

"Don't take other people's troubles too seriously, my dear; try to understand how much being used to things means. If those darkies had to live in your house they'd never rest till they got it as dirty and broken up as what they're used to. Then they'd be comfortable. They like what they've got: they're made that way."

I considered this comfortable doctrine in silence. Then:

"Why didn't God make them another way
—some clean way? It would have been just
as easy."

"That's too deep water for a person of
your inches," he replied. "You must take
God and folks like you find them. But that
little darkey has as much fun as you do—
maybe more: don't worry your head over
nonsense."

A year or two afterwards my father's business took us to a great city of the North; and
I was soon hard at work, on Saturdays and
Sundays, at a church mission in the tenement district. Not content with the class
work at the chapel I visited my small pupils
in their—no, not their homes; I could never
call them that; their dens. There were long
stairs slippery with dirt, where blows and
curses from the foul, dark rooms assailed my
ears; there were rooms with one tiny window,
and rooms with no window at all; there were
beds and tubs and stoves and sewing-ma-
chines and babies and rags and tin cans and
children and dirt and noise in one horrible
confusion.

My mother was dead, and I kept my expe-
ditions to myself. But I turned back to what
my cousin had said about the Negroes for
comfort. Did these white people like the

way they lived? Were they made that way too?

The more I saw of them the more dubious I became; but my sociological researches, becoming known to the family, were summarily put a stop to. So I dropped the biological method and took to books.

But through those early experiences I came unconsciously to regard slum-dwellers as of one class. There were people of many races in those tenements; but their differences sank out of sight before the common degradation of their lives. And always with the thought of these came the memory of that Negro woman and her not-yet stolid child. They were human too; and there was something in them deeper than being Negroes—something that was kin to these emigrants of the tenements, and to me, and to all the world. They were a part of human life, like the rest: their fundamental needs and their fundamental reactions to environment were the same in kind. Whatever differences existed, they were differences in degree.

It is this recognition of human oneness that opens the door of understanding into the Negro slums. One slum interprets another; each slum-dweller helps to explain all the rest, whatever their nationality, wherever

their abode. We can see this when we get
rid of the deadening influence of the old
political economy, and recognize the Negro
slum for what it, and all slums, are—the joint
product of ignorance, greed, and the mon-
strous old doctrine of *laissez faire*.

The old political economy was a science of
investigation, not one of construction, and
still less one at all concerned with morality.
It observed the methods of human business
intercourse much as one might examine the
ways of earthquakes, or any other natural phe-
nomena, with a view to deducting therefrom
certain fixed laws as inherent in the nature
of things, and as unmoral, as the attraction of
oxygen and hydrogen. Thus, for example,
the old doctrine concerning wages—that the
employer would inevitably drive the workman
as close to the edge of starvation as he possibly could while still keeping him alive to
work; and that the workman would resist as
much as he dared with the fear of losing his
job before his eyes—was accepted as a basal
law of a world where, apparently, whatever
was was right. In such a world, the law of
gravitation was no firmer or more respectable
a fixture than the law that the landlord should
get the highest rent he could for the cheapest
shelter the poor could be induced to accept.

The watchword of the old political economy was that business is business—a territory roped off from human considerations, and governed by laws of its own. When human beings got into this district they were subject to the law of the land, which gave a chance only to him who could snatch and hold it. Religion and philanthropy might stand without if they would, and more or less liberally anoint the wounds of those who were worsted in the struggle, but otherwise they had no concern in the fray.

This conception of human relations had governed the world for ages before Ricardo formulated his "iron law." Its mark is deep in our life and thought to-day ; and nowhere is it plainer, the world around, than upon the houses of the poor. In all countries where there is enough of civilization for society to have become divided into groups, the poorer folk, often without a sense of wrong on their part or injustice on the landlords', have been huddled together in a manner to bring property-owners the largest returns, regardless of other consequences.

Those other consequences have none the less left their mark also deep in human life. They are the same everywhere, regardless of country or race.

Cleanliness of body and of habitation is a fundamental preparation for cleanliness of mind, and water and fresh air exist in abundance to furnish it; yet the houses of those who most need cleanliness, and to whom it is most difficult by inclination and occupation, are largely cut off from these two necessities without which human life cannot be normal. A well-to-do child, with generations of bath-tubs, outdoor sports, and sunny rooms behind him, might retain through life moral and even physical health under the conditions of the world's slums; but his children would show signs of breaking; and their children would be as truly of the slum as their neighbours. Generations of gain could be lost in one man's lifetime. Yet of the mass of the Negroes, who live in the slums we have built for them, where water is hard to come by and adequate ventilation impossible, we say that they are dirty by nature, and that to provide better things would result only in a waste of money.

We know little, as yet, in this our dawn of social consciousness, of the slums of the rest of the world. Our slum-dwellers are to us a race apart, a separate fragment of life, unrelated, a law unto themselves. They make their slums, we think, as a spider spins his web, from within. We all know, of course, that very many Negroes are far above the slum-dwellers. There are few communities in the South, however small, without a few Negroes whom the whites respect and trust. But we regard them, not as the natural outcome of a more normal chance in life, but as exceptions to the law of Negro development, through some personally-inherent exceptional quality, probably an infusion of white blood.

We need a wide horizon for the understanding of our slum-dweller. When we set him in his world-relations we see that in all mankind slum conditions produce slum results. Waterless, ill-ventilated houses, crowded beyond the possibility of decency because of low wages and high rents, make impossible the physical basis that is necessary for even the poorest home. And with this kind of housing go other evils, all working together to produce in any people, the world around, those characteristics which we believe to be racial and Negro. In a population racially homogeneous, like that of Rome or of Pekin, or racially heterogeneous like that of Chicago or New York, or in a bi-racial population like our own, the results are the same. Bad housing conditions, insufficient or un-nourishing food, vicious surroundings, a childhood spent unprotected in the streets, produce, in Europe, Asia, and America, ill-nourished bodies, unbalanced nerves, vacant and vicious minds, a craving for stimulants and all evil excitements, lack of energy, weakened wills, laziness, thriftlessness, unreliability in every relation of life.

As life rises, it differentiates. Anglo-Saxon and Chinaman develop along different lines; and the higher their development the less alike they are. Each brings his own race-contribution to the great Race of Man. But in those lowest depths, where men are thrust back towards the level of beasts, acquired characteristics are in abeyance, and the old brute longings dominate once more. Men are wonderfully alike on this level—as alike as are vegetable and animal on their lowest plane: and yellow or white or black, there is little for any to boast of. But when normal conditions of growth are furnished, men of each race will come true to type; and the higher they rise the greater their differences will be. Just what the highest type of the Negro race will be nobody knows; for as a race they have not yet had normal conditions, nor time for full development. But whatever it may be, it will not be a white type, nor a red nor a yellow one ; and it will be something needed for the perfect development of the Race of Man.

These things being so—and a wide world-look is convincing—the places where our poorest live, our weakest and most tempted folk, take on new aspects and suggest new implications. Our slums are not the product of a race unrelated and incapable of development ; they are our part of a world-wide morass where life capable of higher things is sucked under and destroyed.

The old political economy took no account of such matters ; it accepted as a universal law the policy of exploitation, of individualistic commercialism, of cut-throat competition. It saw, not human beings, but profit and loss.

The new political economy is shifting the thought and the business of the world towards a basis of human brotherhood. It puts human rights above profit and loss, and holds conservation a wiser policy than exploitation. As to the human morass, it would drain it. And all this not as a matter of charity, not because Christ said men are all brethen ; but because we *are* all brethren, and so lose more than we gain, in the long run, if we run things on any other basis. That thing Christ said is true !

When one sees in the slum-dweller a brother, what is one to do ? If he really is a brother it will pay to treat him like one. Laws—the real ones—never do contradict one another. No law of true prosperity can be infringed upon by obedience to the law of brotherhood, if brotherhood is a real fact. It will work with any other real law there is.

A woman saw that, fifty years ago, and set out to demonstrate it in this very matter of housing.

" The people's homes are bad," she wrote, " partly because they are badly built and arranged ; they are tenfold worse because the tenants' habits and lives are what they are. Transplant them to-morrow to healthy and commodious homes, and they would pollute and destroy them. There needs, and will need for some time, a reformatory work which will demand that loving zeal of individuals which cannot be legislated for by parliament. The heart of the English nation will supply it. It may and should be organized ; it cannot be created."

Might not that have been written of the very poor of New York or St. Louis, instead of the very poor of London ? Or of the very poor of Atlanta or Birmingham, who happen to be black ?

In 1866, three years after Ruskin's three thousand pounds made the beginning of her work possible, Miss Hill wrote again :

"That the spiritual elevation of a large class depended to a considerable extent on sanitary reform was, I considered, proved. But I was equally certain that sanitary improvement itself was dependent on educational work among grown-up people. . . . It seems to me that a greater power is in the hands of landlords and landladies than of school-teachers—power either of life or death, physical and spiritual.

"The disciplining of our immense poor population must be effected by individual influence ; and this power can change it from a mob of paupers and semi-paupers into a body of self-dependent workers."

It can change it because it did, and does ; and Mr. Ruskin, "who alone believed the scheme would work," was repaid in good English money for his investment, as were the many others whose renting properties she and her trained assistants managed during the fifty years between her first experiment in 1863 and her death in 1912.

After twenty years of work she wrote, in 1883 :

"I have no hesitation in saying that if a

site were handed over to me at the [usual]
price, I would engage to house upon it under
thoroughly healthy conditions, at rents which
they could pay, and which would yield a fair
interest on capital, a very large proportion of
the very poor."

And what was Miss Hill's scheme? Just a
combination of the law of brotherhood with a
sound business policy in collecting rents.
With Ruskin's money she acquired three
houses "in a dreadful state of dirt and neglect." This was remedied, and an ample
water supply provided. She herself undertook to collect the weekly rent. At first her
tenants regarded her as a natural enemy.
Sometimes, when she went on Saturday
nights for her rent, she found them lying on
their filthy floors, dead drunk. The rent
would often be thrust out to her through a
crack in the door, held fast against her en-
trance. The stairs were "many inches deep
in dirt, so hardened that a shovel had to be
used to get it off." The people were the
poorest renting class, just above vagrants;
they lived on the edge of crime, and all too frequently passed over the fatal line. "Truly,"
said Miss Hill, "a wild, lawless, desolate little
kingdom to rule over."

"On what principles was I to rule these

people? On the same that I had already tried, and tried with success, in other places, and which I may sum up as the two following: firstly, to demand a strict fulfillment of their duties to me—one of the chief of which would be the punctual payment of rent; and secondly, to endeavour to be so unfailingly just and patient, that they should learn to trust the rule that was over them.

"With regard to details, I would make a few improvements at once—such, for example, as the laying on of water and repairing of dust bins; but, for the most part, improvements should be made only by degrees, as the people became more capable of valuing and not abusing them. I would have the rooms distempered and thoroughly cleansed as they became vacant, and then they should be offered to the more cleanly of the tenants. I would save such repairs as were not immediately needed as a means of giving work to the men in times of distress. I would draft the occupants of the underground kitchens into the up-stairs rooms, and would ultimately convert the kitchens into bath-rooms and wash-houses. I would have the landlady's portion of the house—*i. e.*, the stairs and passages—at once repaired and distempered; and they should be regularly

scrubbed, and, as far as possible, made
models of cleanliness ; for I knew from former
experience that the example of this would, in
time, silently spread itself to the rooms themselves, and that payment for this work would
give me some hold over the elder girls.   I
would collect savings personally, not trust to
their being taken to distant banks or saving
clubs.   And, finally, I knew that I should
learn to feel these people as my friends, and
so should instinctively feel the same respect
for their privacy and their independence, and
should treat them with the same courtesy,
that I should show towards any other personal friends.   There would be no interference, no entering their rooms uninvited, no
offer of money or the necessaries of life.   But
when occasion presented itself I should give
them any help I could, such as I might offer
without insult to other friends—sympathy in
their distresses ; advice, help, and counsel in
their difficulties.   .   .   .

" When we set about our repairs and alter-
ations, there was much that was discourag-
ing.   The better class of people in the court
were hopeless of any permanent improvement.   When one of the tenants of the shops
saw that we were sending workmen into the
empty rooms, he said considerately, 'I'll tell

AN ALABAMA SCHOOL IMPROVEMENT LEAGUE.

A GEORGIA COUNTY SUPERINTENDENT VISITING
NEGRO SCHOOL.

104B

you what it is, Miss, it'll cost you a lot o' money to repair them places, and it's no good. The women's 'eads'll be druv through the door panels again in no time, and the place is good enough for such cattle as them there.'   But we were not to be deterred.

"On the other hand, we were not to be hurried in our action by threats. These were not wanting. For no sooner did the tenants see the workmen about than they seemed to think that if they only clamoured enough, they would get their own rooms put to rights. Nothing had been done for years. Now, they thought, was their opportunity. More than one woman locked me in her room with her, the better to rave and storm. She would shake the rent in her pocket to tempt me with the sound of the money, and roar out ' that never a farthing of it would she pay till her grate was set,' or her floor was mended, as the case might be. Perfect silence would make her voice drop lower and lower, until at last she would stop, wondering that no violent answers were hurled back at her, and a pause would ensue. I felt that promises would be little believed in, and besides, I wished to feel free to do as much, and only as much, as seemed to me best ; so that my plan was to trust to my deeds to speak for themselves, and inspire confidence as time went on.

" The importance of advancing slowly, and of gaining some hold over the people as a necessary accompaniment to any real improvement in their dwellings, was perpetually apparent.  Their habits were so degraded that we had to work a change in these before they would make any proper use of the improved surroundings we were prepared to give them.  We had locks torn off, windows broken, drains stopped, dust-bins misused in every manner ; even pipes broken, and water-taps wrenched away.  This was sometimes the result of carelessness, and a deeply-rooted habit of dirt and untidiness ; sometimes the damage was willful.  Our remedy was to watch the right moment for furnishing these appliances, to persevere in supplying them, and to get the people by degrees to work with us for their preservation.  I have learned to know that people are ashamed to abuse a place they find cared for.  They will add dirt to dirt till a place is pestilential, but the more they find done for it, the more they will respect it, till at last order and cleanliness prevail.  It is this feeling of theirs, coupled with the fact that they do not like those whom they have learned to love, and whose standard is higher than their own, to see things which would grieve them, which has enabled us to accomplish nearly every reform of outward things that we have achieved ; so that the surest way to have any place kept clean is to go through it often yourself.  .  .  .

" I mentioned our custom of using some of the necessary, yet not immediately wanted repairs as a means of affording work to tenants in slack times.  .  .  .  When a tenant is out of work, instead of reducing his energy by any gifts of money, we simply, whenever the funds at our disposal allow it, employ him in restoring and purifying the houses. And what a difference five shillings' worth of work in a bad week will make to a family ! The father, instead of idling listlessly at the corner of the street, sets busily and happily to work, prepares the whitewash, mends the plaster, distempers the room ; the wife bethinks herself of having a turn-out of musty corners or drawers—untouched, maybe, for months—of cleaning her windows, perhaps even of putting up a clean blind ; and thus a sense of decency, the hope of beginning afresh and doing better, comes like new life into the home.

" The same cheering and encouraging sort of influence, though in a less degree, is exercised by our plan of having a little band of scrubbers.

" We have each passage scrubbed twice a week by one of the elder girls.  The sixpence thus earned is a stimulus, and they often take an extreme interest in the work itself.  One little girl was so proud of her first cleaning that she stood two hours watching her passage lest the boys, whom she considered as the natural enemies of order and cleanliness, should spoil it before I came to see it.  And one woman remarked to her neighbour how nice the stairs looked.  ' They haven't been cleaned,' she added, 'since ever I came into this house.'  She had been there six years! The effect of these clean passages frequently spreads to the rooms, as the dark line of demarcation between the cleaned passage and the still dirty room arouses the attention, and begins to trouble the minds of its inmates.

"Gradually, then, these various modes of dealing with our little realm began to tell. Gradually the people began to trust us ; and gradually the houses were improved.  The sense of quiet power and sympathy soon made itself felt, and less and less was there any sign of rudeness or violence towards ourselves.  Even before the first winter was over many a one would hurry to light us up the stairs, and instead of my having the rent-book and money thrust to me through the half-open door, my reception would be, ' Oh, can't you come in, Miss, and sit down for a bit?' Little by little houses were renovated, the grates reset, the holes in the floors repaired, the cracking, dirty plaster replaced by a clean, smooth surface, the heaps of rubbish removed, and we progressed towards order.

"Amongst the many benefits which the possession of the houses enables us to confer on the people, perhaps one of the most important, is our power of saving them from neighbours who would render their lives miserable. It is a most merciful thing to protect the poor from the pain of living in the next room to drunken, disorderly people. ' I am dying,' said an old woman to me the other day : ' I wish you would put me where I can't hear S—— beating his wife. Her screams are awful. And B——, too, he do come in so drunk. Let me go over the way to No. 30.' Our success depends on duly arranging the inmates : not too many children in any one house, so as to overcrowd it ; not too few, so as to overcrowd another ; not two bad people side by side, or they drink together ; not a terribly bad person beside a very respectable one.   .   .   .

" On Saturday evenings, about eight o'clock, the tenants know that we are to be found in the club-room . . . and that they may come to us there if they like, either for business or a friendly chat.

" Picture a low, rather long room, one of my assistants and myself sitting in state, with pen and ink and bags for money at a deal table under a flaring gas-jet ; the door, which leads straight into the court, standing wide open.  A bright red blind, drawn down over the broad window, prevents the passers-by from gazing in there, but round the open door there are gathered a set of wild, dirty faces looking in upon us.  Such a semicircle they make, as the strong gas-light falls upon them !  They are mostly children with di- shevelled hair, and ragged, uncared-for clothes ; but above them, now and then, one sees the haggard face of a woman hurrying to make her Saturday evening purchases, or the vacant stare of some half-drunken man. The grown-up people who stop to look in are usually strangers, for those who know us generally come in to us.  ' Well ! they give it this time, anyhow,' one woman will exclaim, sitting down on a bench near us, so engrossed in the question of whether she obtains a par- ish allowance that she thinks ' they ' can mean no one but the Board of Guardians, and ' it' nothing but the much-desired allowance. 'Yes, I thought I'd come in and tell you,' she will go on ; 'I went up Tuesday ——' And then will follow the whole story.

" ' Well, and how do you find yourself, Miss ?' a big Irish labourer in a flannel jacket will say, entering afterwards ; 'I just come in to say I shall be knocked off Monday ; finished a job across the park : and if so be there's any little thing in whitewashing to do, why, I'll be glad to do it.'

" ' Presently,' we reply, nodding to a thin, slight woman at the door. She has not spoken, but we know the meaning of that beseeching look. She wants us to go up and get her husband's rent from him before he goes out to spend more of it in drink.

" The eager, watchful eyes of one of our little scrubbers next attract attention : there she stands, with her savings-card in her hand, waiting till we enter the sixpences she has earned from us during the week. 'How much have I got ?' she says, eyeing the written sixpences with delight, ' because mother says, please, I'm to draw out next Saturday ; she's going to buy me a pair of boots.'

" ' Take two shillings on the card and four

shillings rent,' a proudly happy woman will say, as she lays down a piece of bright gold. A rare sight this in the court, but her husband has been in regular work for some little time.

" ' Please, Miss,' says another woman, ' will you see and do something for Jane? She's that masterful since her father died, I can't do nothing with her, and she'll do no good in this court. Do see and get her a place somewheres away.'

" A man will enter now: ' I'll leave you my rent to-night, Miss, instead o' Monday, please; it'll be safer with you than with me.'

" A pale woman comes next, in great sorrow. Her husband, she tells us, has been arrested without cause. We believe this to be true; the man has always paid his way honestly, worked industriously, and lived decently. So my assistant goes round to the police-station at once to bail him, while I remain to collect the savings. ' Did he seem grateful?' I say to her on her return. ' He took it very quietly,' is her answer; ' he seemed to feel it quite natural that we should help him.'

" Such are some of the scenes on our savings evenings; such some of the services we are called upon to render; such the kind of footing we are on with our tenants. An evening such as this assuredly shows that our footing has somewhat changed since those spent in this court during the first winter.

" My readers will not imagine that I mean to imply that there are not still depths of evil remaining in this court. It would be impossible for such a place as I described it as being originally to be raised in two years to a satisfactory condition. But what I do contend is, that we have worked some very real reforms, and seen some very real results. I feel that it is in a very great degree a question of time, and that, now that we have got hold of the hearts of the people, the court is sure to improve steadily. It will pay as good a percentage to its owners, and will benefit its tenants as much, as any of the other properties under my management have done. This court contains two out of eight properties on which the same plans have been tried, and all of them are increasingly prosperous. The first two were purchased by Mr. Ruskin.

"It appears to me then to be proved by practical experience that when we can induce the rich to undertake the duties of landlord in poor neighbourhoods, and ensure a suffi-

cient amount of the wise, personal supervision of educated and sympathetic people
acting as their representatives, we achieve
results which are not attainable in any other
way.  .  .  .  It is not so much a question
of dealing with houses alone, as of dealing
with houses in connection with their influence
on the character and habits of the people who
inhabit them.  .  .  .  The principle on which
the whole work rests is that the inhabitants
and their surroundings must be improved
together.    It has never yet failed to succeed.

" Finally, I would call upon those who may
possess cottage property in large towns to
consider the immense power they thus hold
in their hands, and the large influence for
good they may exercise by the wise use
of that power.  .  .  .  And I would ask
those who do not hold such property to consider whether they might not, by possessing
themselves of some, confer lasting benefits on
their poorer neighbours ?

" In these pages I have dwelt mainly on
the way our management affects the people,
as I have given elsewhere my experience as
to financial matters and details of practical
management.  But I may here urge one
thing on those about to undertake to deal
with such property—the extreme importance

of enforcing the punctual payment of rents. This principle is a vital one. Firstly, because it strikes one blow at the credit system, that curse of the poor; secondly, because it prevents large losses from bad debts, and prevents the tenant from believing he will be suffered to remain, whatever his conduct may be, resting that belief on his knowledge of the large sum that would be lost were he turned out; and, thirdly, because the mere fact that the man is kept up to his duty is a help to him, and increases his self-respect and hope of doing better.

"I would also say to those who, in the carrying out of such an undertaking, are brought into immediate contact with the tenants, that its success will depend most of all on their giving sympathy to the tenants, and awakening confidence in them; but it will depend also in a great degree on their power of bestowing concentrated attention on small details. . . .

"It is the small things of the world that colour the lives of those around, and it is on persistent efforts to reform these that progress depends; and we may rest assured that they who see with greater eyes than ours have a due estimate of the service, and that if we did but perceive the mighty principles

underlying these tiny things we should rather
feel awed that we are entrusted with them at
all, than scornful and impatient that they are
no larger. What are we that we should
ask for more than that God should let us work
for Him among the tangible things which He
created to be fair, and the human spirits
which He redeemed to be pure?"

I have quoted at length from Miss Hill's
little book, partly because her work is so little known in the South; partly because her
own words make so clear the basis of human
sympathy on which the success of all such
work must depend. That sympathy is a
world-principle, a world-need, and a world-
power. If she proved with these people—as
she did for fifty years—that business success is entirely compatible with a spirit of
brotherhood; that housing reform and the
reform of immorality and vice go hand in
hand; that paupers and semi-paupers can
be changed into a body of self-dependent
workers; then surely there is hope for slum-
dwellers elsewhere.

The Octavia Hill plan has been tried in a
number of cities in England and Scotland;
and in New York, Boston, and Philadelphia.
The work has been to a remarkable degree
both financially and humanly successful.

Mme. Montessori's work in Rome is among this same tenement class. Her Houses of Childhood are in re-made tenements, where good business and brotherhood go hand in hand. The children who have astonished the world are from this same class of paupers, semi-paupers and criminals. Until opportunity was offered these who had been denied it, who could have guessed the measure of their response?

The Negroes of this same economic class need what their class needs the world around. They will respond in the same way. The colour of one's skin, or even the shape of one's head, cannot change the working of a principle. The trouble in lifting up this lowest class of Negroes is that we have not yet paid the price. Things worth doing always cost ; and to do this thing among us will take, in somebody's heart, that same passion for justice and opportunity for the weak that it takes everywhere else.

But the doing of it need not wait until that passion rises in all hearts, else one might well despair. Prove that a thing pays—in money—and it goes. Men and women who cared little for humanity were glad to turn the management of their tenement property over to Miss Hill as soon as they found returns by her methods were better than by theirs. She was so overwhelmed with offers that she and her assistants had to refuse much of what the owners urged upon them. Many of the great manufacturers of this and other countries frankly admit that their reason for the extensive welfare work they carry on among their working people is purely a business one : they have found that it pays, in money, to care for " the human end of the machine."

That is the way the world moves. The people with love in their hearts, the seers, pay the price, open the new way, and prove it better than the old ; then people walk in it, because it is proven good.

There is nothing to do with many of the shanties for Negroes, in city and country, but to condemn them by law and tear them down. As our social conscience becomes aroused this will inevitably be done. Many houses now in use would do very well if given a water supply and some extra windows, provided the rent-collecting were done, not by an indifferent or contemptuous real estate agent, but on the Octavia Hill plan.

Negro women of force and character should be trained under white auspices to do this work. Two or three owners of Negro rent-

ing property could together employ such a
rent collector for what the real estate agent
would cost, or less. Their property would
improve as well as their tenants ; and the
frightful waste of humanity that goes on in
our slums, the drifting of wreckage into prisons and poorhouses, would not only be
checked, but these now broken creatures
would become a community asset, as every
real worker is.

We need an experiment station in the housing of Negroes of this class. An ordinary
city block, two-thirds of it covered with decent
little houses, could carry the interest on the
whole investment, though one-third be given
over to a playground, on a corner of which
should stand a community house with rooms
for clubs and industrial classes, as well as a
decent meeting place for young people in the
evening. Such a plant would demonstrate
that healthful housing of the very poor could
be made a paying investment ; and the income from it, if made available for such a
purpose, would provide for the training, under the best of white management, of the
Negro social workers so sorely needed in the
homes of our poor.

Calls for such workers are already coming
from white people in several Southern states.

The owner of a lumber camp in the Southwest, who has long carried on welfare work among his white employees, has tried to get a Negro woman to help his coloured employees; and similar efforts have been lately made by several others. A Southern white woman wrote me recently of conditions in a camp of Negroes where electricity was being developed from water power. The workmen had their families with them—fourteen hundred black folk in all, herded like cattle there in God's clean mountains, and living as untaught, helpless people will. Drinking, vice, and immorality were rampant. The women knew nothing of home-making, had homes been possible. The children were born like flies, and grew or died in moral and physical filth. A breeding-place for criminals! And the right kind of Negro woman, properly trained, and backed by a corporation merely selfishly intelligent, could have brought outward order and decency, lifted the workers to a far higher efficiency, and created many real homes there, each one a point of contagion for life and hope and health. It would pay in dollars and cents.

It is impossible to speak of housing for Negroes without a word about the better classes among them, and the fight these must make for decent homes.

The thrifty working people, who constitute a large and ever-growing class, make heroic sacrifices to own their own homes. This is easier to do in the country than in the city, and the home, when won, is far safer; for if one owns even a very few acres one need not fear the placing of a saloon next door, or a low dance-hall, or a vice resort for white people—evils which constantly threaten every Negro owner of a hard-won city home. Sanitary conditions, too, are under one's own control, and with intelligent parents it is possible for children to grow up in robust health, which they can scarcely do in those parts of our cities open to Negro homes. The country is the place for poor Negroes, not because they are Negroes, but because they are human, and of like needs with the rest of the world.

But before they will be permanently content in the country they must have what any race of people must have under like conditions : perfect security for life and property ; and such education as will relate them to country life in an efficient, social and joyful way.

Neither of these things is beyond attainment. The trend towards better education in the Negro rural schools is noted elsewhere ; and the effects of this movement will be powerfully reinforced by the decision of the United States Government to use its eight hundred Southern farm-demonstrators for work among both races. There is also a strong element in the Southern state universities which favours the inclusion of gatherings of Negro farmers in the agricultural extension work of their lecturers and demonstrators. When these things bear fruit, and when not merely a large part of the South, but absolutely all of it, is as safe for Negroes as for white people, the housing of the country Negro will be a problem practically solved.

The city 'dwellers are in a harder case. The poorest share the fate of slum-dwellers of all races. They live in those sections which are morally and physically the least desirable, and are neglected habitually by the city health authorities. Cleanliness and decency are alike beyond them. But in addition to these things, in far too many of our cities, both the respectable working man and the prosperous, educated Negro are forced to live in surroundings from which men of any other race, of their economic status, would be allowed to escape.

It is even worse than that. When by their own efforts a few Negroes secure a respectable neighbourhood, families of the better class building up a little community of their own, they are peculiarly liable to have saloons and houses of ill-fame thrust upon them by a low class of whites whom the upper classes do not restrain. The Negro owner of a city home, whatever his education or business success, whatever the sum invested in his property, cannot be sure, from month to month, of retaining for his family surroundings compatible with moral health and safety.

I know a Negro, an honour graduate of Brown University, a winner there of the fellowship in the American School at Athens, Greece. He is a man of wide attainments, of blameless life, of modesty and good manners. He is in full sympathy with the best Southern thought concerning race relations ; and his wide influence among his people is a thing for white Southerners to be thankful for. He has turned aside from money-getting, all these years, to serve his people in return for a very simple living. By what effort one can imagine he bought a little home. It is far from his work, on the outskirts of the city, placed there in the hope that his children might grow up in safety.

His home attracted other homes, until the neighbourhood became good enough for a white man's house of ill-fame, which he found was to be erected on the lot adjoining his own. He has three daughters, the oldest barely grown. He saved himself by buying the lot, at a cost of long saving and strain.

"But I am not safe any more," he said. "There are still vacant lots there; and I can't possibly buy them all."

If I were a Negro I should do just as Negroes do—resent with all my heart our stupid white assumption that when they attempt to buy property in our own desirable sections they are trying to force themselves upon us in impudence, and to assert their belief in and desire for "social equality."

What these Negroes of the better classes want is first of all a neighbourhood of assured moral decency in which to rear their children. Their passionate desire for character in their children we do not begin to understand. Next to that they want sanitary conditions, and avoidance of the lower classes of their own people, just as we do ourselves. To get these things some Negroes are willing to thrust themselves, if they can, among white people, and to endure their resentment and contempt.

"If you white people could only understand!" a Negro woman said to me not long
ago, her face fired with feeling. "We don't
want our homes where we're not wanted.
But we want to be decent, too. And it's the
same all over the country—anything will do
for a 'nigger.' You think we're all alike, and
you don't care what happens to us just so
we're out of your sight. My husband and I
were living in Denver; and we had money
to pay for a comfortable house. But there
wasn't a place for rent to Negroes that a self-
respecting Negro would have. And how will
my people ever learn to be decent if they
must live in the white people's vice district?"

We have no right to treat people like that.
In one large Southern city, with high taxes
and a big revenue and an expensive health
department, a white friend of mine counted
one morning twelve dead cats and dogs, in
various stages of decomposition, in one short
Negro alley. It was not an uncommon sight,
except that the corpses were rather numerous.
The outhouses are vile beyond description, a
menace not merely to the Negroes but to the
entire community. Yet if a Negro tries to
buy a home in a healthful part of town we
think his one motive is to thrust himself
upon us, socially, just as far as he dares.

The way out of a situation like that is so simple, so plain! What is needed to solve the problem is not a segregation law, to force those who would be clean back into the bog we ought to drain out of existence ; it is just to put ourselves in the Negroes' place and do as we would be done by. If we white people could only have a Negro's consciousness for a day or two it would clear up so many things. As it is, we can at least use our imagination.

If the city's health laws were enforced where they are most needed, punishing those who break them if necessary, till they learned better ; if streets could be set aside in a district capable of being made attractive, and a fair share of city improvements put there ; if the Negroes who built good homes there were protected as well-to-do white people are from the fear of saloons and other vice resorts ; if it were all done not in contempt, but in a spirit of justice and human consideration, there would be no need for segregation laws. Negroes, like white people, like to live among their friends. The overwhelming majority of them believe, as we do, in the social separation of the races ; and beyond that, they do not want their children to grow up among those who look down upon them.

I am told that a well-to-do Negro in Kansas City, understanding his people's feeling, bought a considerable tract of land there, some distance out, and improved it as white men do for white buyers. The lots were sold under restrictions which guaranteed the neighbourhood morally, and went, my informant said, "like hot cakes." The place is to-day the most desirable for Negro home-owners in Kansas City. The man who bought the land originally made a handsome profit. His example could be followed by real estate men, white or black, in any large Southern city with an assurance of success. It is really not bad business to do justice.

I have dwelt at length on this matter of Negro homes because it is fundamental to justice, and therefore to any lasting adjustment between the races. No people can rise higher than their homes. And we criticize unsparingly the Negro's weakness and faults, yet fasten upon him living conditions which, the world over and among all races, breed just those things for which we blame him most.

## IV

### AN OUNCE OF PREVENTION

THERE is practical unanimity in the South regarding the low moral standards of the Negro race as a whole. We admit that there are exceptions to the rule ; we always know a few personally. But the overwhelming concensus of opinion is that Negroes generally are dirty, untruthful, and immoral; and beyond and above and below everything else, they are by nature dishonest.

However exaggerated such statements may be as applied to the whole ten million Negroes in America, very many of whom are practically as unknown to us whites as though they lived in another country, they are dangerously true of a large part of that class with which we come most frequently in contact. But have we ever asked ourselves why ? Have we gone into their homes to find what drives them ? Do we know anything of the wants in their lives ? Have we any idea of the tremendous forces of wreckage which gather in those great empty places where human need cries with none to answer ?

If we would look a little into the lives of those who live below the poverty line in communities where there are no black people, we would find that there is a certain degree of pressure under which human character, in the mass, tends to break. The ideal of humanity is the man who will meet all tests, endure all pressure, surmount all difficulties, suffer all loss, and pass out at last still pure in heart, unspotted, undefiled. However we fail ourselves—nay, because we fail—we cling to this ideal as the standard by which men should be judged. Whatever soil of sin be on us, we know, in our inmost hearts, that men and women were meant to be like that. It is for this that we honour our heroes and martyrs, who, wherever they have come to birth, belong first of all to humanity, and not to any one race. It is not for what they bore that we love them most, nor for what they have achieved : they are to us revealers of our own possibilities. We see in them the heights to which we ourselves, and all humanity, were meant to rise.

But is a child's power of resistance to be tested like an adult's ? We are learning that premature burdens will strain young muscle beyond the possibility of future vigour.  We found out long ago that young colts and calves must be shielded from undue strain : we lost money unless they were.

Later, and more slowly, the world is waking to the money loss involved in straining children's muscles too soon.  We find that a child's muscles are a national asset, or ought to be, as well as a colt's.  But character is a more precious asset still.  It is a driving-force scarcely to be measured in national life, a productive source of wealth, as well as of happiness, beyond any other one thing.  It is of far slower growth than muscle, and strain is more fatal, care more vital to it.  Even the highest races are still so undeveloped morally that in any heavy, widespread stress the cartilaginous honour of thousands will give under the pressure, until men hitherto counted blameless seem little better than beasts.  Times of war disclose conditions like that, invariably ; and times of wide-spread panic, or famine, or disaster of any kind.  The San Francisco earthquake furnished a recent and spectacular example.

Now when these things are true of favoured folk, of those who have had something of a normal chance in life, we may be sure, even before we look to see, that those cut off from

PLAYGROUND AT STORY HOUR, LOUISVILLE.

130B

a normal chance will not, in the mass, develop much power of resistance to undue strain. They, of all men, have least to bear strain with. Their moral muscles, under-nourished and over-strained from birth, are uncoördinated with one another, or with their wills. The will itself hangs loose and undeveloped, shaken by vagrant desires and passing storms of passion. These are the people, the world around, who strew the path of civilization with wreckage. Crime is but the extreme manifestation of conditions which create vast swamps of incapacity, shiftlessness and immorality, in which human character is engulfed as in a quicksand, and out of which crime emerges as the topmost blossom of its rank and fetid growth.

What are some of the main causes of this human ruin and waste? Not here in the South, but everywhere. We have no peculiar laws of life down here, any more than we have peculiar laws of physics. If an apple falls to the ground in England because of the attraction of gravitation, one will fall in Maine, or in Georgia, or in Kamchatka, for exactly the same reason. And if certain conditions in New York wreck physical and moral health in human beings, and result in all unhuman ruin, those same conditions will produce similar results, in any climate, upon any fragment of humanity exposed to them.

We are a pious people here in the South— perhaps, like our brethren elsewhere, more pious than we are Christlike. There are very many of us who, when the effect of conditions on character is asserted, begin at once to defend God's almightiness, and the power of grace to save to the uttermost. To some among us it seems a reflection on grace to suggest that men ever need anything else, or need grace itself anywhere but in their own lives. But they do need it elsewhere, nevertheless—in the hearts and lives of other people, and expressed in the conditions which surround them. One of the best women I know, one of unusual intelligence and education, said to me not long ago, in a hesitating, doubtful voice :

" And you heard her say, that doctor, just as I did, that when she examined the blood of those thirty fallen girls the average for the thirty was less than three million red blood-corpuscles where five million were normal ; and that blood so impoverished lowered the vitality, starved the nerves, lessened their resistive power to temptation and impaired their wills, as well as their energy and ability to work. She said they were not fallen

women : they were felled women—felled by
social conditions to which we Christian women
assented.—It did sound reasonable, I know,
and dreadful. I felt like a criminal myself, almost. But doesn't it leave out God, and salvation ? Where does sin come in when you
look at society like that? And surely God is
almighty ; and His grace ——." She looked
at me, a puzzled frown between her eyes.

I do not doubt God's almightiness ; nor do
I pretend to understand why, being almighty,
He has chosen to so limit His own power that
His own will cannot possibly get done in this
world until men are willing to do it. I do
not doubt that He can do a great many things
which I feel sure He never will. He never will,
for instance, enable a man to make two hundred bushels of corn to the acre on land un-
cleared of weeds : and He will not return to
any people, or any church, a harvest of
"saved souls" in bodies whose living conditions defy all His laws of health and growth
and decency, moral and physical. A few ears
of corn may come to maturity, even among
the weeds ; and a man or woman here or
there may rise to newness of life despite
surroundings which deal death on every
side : but the law holds good, all the same.
It would be quite as effective, and fully as

religious, so far as I can understand, to
kneel beside the untouched weeds and pray
for a bumper crop of corn as it is for us
Christians to pray for the souls' salvation of
the poor, and go comfortably home to din-
ner without one rudimentary intention of
furnishing them surroundings in which love
and righteousness can flourish.  To look at
community life like that does not, to my mind,
do away with sin.  It fixes it on us, the supposedly righteous, who know and do not,
rather than on those who neither know nor
do, and whom we fail to enlighten or protect.

I know the feeling is very strong in the
South against any attempt at regeneration
by man-made law instead of by spiritual
processes ; and I would not seem to fail in
reverence to that best and greatest of all
miracles, the redeeming life of God in the
soul.  I believe, in the brave words of Dr.
Wines, spoken at the International Prison
Congress after forty years of labour for prison
reform, that "reformation is never accom-
plished until the heart has been reached and
regenerated by the grace of Almighty God."
I also believe that our neglect of the living
conditions of the poor has raised barriers between them and that grace which can no
more be removed by prayer alone, or by

faith not "made whole with deed," than weeds could be removed from a corn field by the same process. To destroy those barriers by arousing a community conscience, and recording its awakening in community action expressed in statutory law, is more religious by far than any amount of prayer for the salvation of the poor offered by folk who go home to idleness. We have thrown on the poor, and on God's grace, responsibility for the results of our own sins of neglect : and until the churches shoulder their share of responsibility for community conditions which defy the Bible law of human brotherhood here and now, I do not believe they will make any great headway, in the world outside their borders, in preaching the fatherhood of God or salvation for the world to come.

Where, then, should one apply the hoe in order to earn the right to pray unashamed for a harvest of salvation among the poor ?

The matters of housing and sanitation have been already touched upon ; inadequately, yet enough, I trust, to set wiser minds than my own to thinking, and stronger hands to work. Next to it, and closely connected with it, is the fundamental question of recreation.

The negations of life are the deadly things. Overt acts of wrong have inflicted untold miseries in every age ; yet for blight upon humanity at large they cannot compare with the steady, persistent, accumulated results of perfectly respectable neglects. And the neglect of the human desire for recreation, age-long, world-wide, has been so often not merely respectable, but a virtue of the highest standing ! We have talked much of the universal instinct for God, so evident even among savages ; and we have based on it one of our strongest arguments for the existence of a God : to such universal need, we say, there must be somewhere an answer ; the existence of the need demands it. But in this universal play-instinct, common to all races and all time, we have found no proof of a need that demands an answer, no trace of a wise Creator's handiwork, nothing at all of design. For centuries it was merely an elfish trick of youth, to be as nearly suppressed as possible, being dangerously akin to the devil and all his works. And even now many affectionate and otherwise intelligent parents regard it as a part of their children's childhood and youth merely, to be lived through until that safe stage of maturity be reached where children become sober and sensible, and put away childish things. Many provide dolls and balls because they enjoy giving their children pleasure, but with little idea that the love of play is almost the greatest formative power in a child's life, and that by it he may be shaped to the highest ideals, the widest usefulness, or be degraded to the level of the beast.

It is not merely that a child coördinates his muscles and mind in play ; he coördinates his entire being with the world about him in play that is wisely directed. He finds himself as a citizen of his world. In team-play, in the give and take of success and defeat, in fair play and respect for the rules of the game, he learns self-control, respect for the rights of others, the adjustment of his own personality to those about him, and a deep regard for law and justice.

All these things are fundamental to a law-abiding, honest life. In families of several children, where the mother is willing and able to share the play life of the children, they may learn these things at home, even in cramped quarters and under unfavourable conditions : but few poor children have mothers of leisure. There is no place for their play in the cluttered house, or in the diminutive yard some poor people are fortunate enough to own.  In the cities the streets are the playgrounds of the poor.  They are such for our poor, the Negroes.  There is little play possible there, even in smaller cities, that fits their need.  Besides, few of them know how to play, in city or country.  The play-instinct has been perverted or suppressed so long that its natural outlet, with many of them, seems closed.  They are not peculiar in this : they have simply suffered the deprivation of a deep human need, as children of the very poor have done elsewhere; and they react under the unnatural condition exactly as does all the rest of humanity in a similar situation.

There are certain laws of spiritual physics which are universal in their operation, and which seem closely akin to the physics of matter.  One can compress the air, guide it according to its own laws in prepared channels, and work with it miracles of usefulness.  One can compress it with no outlet at all, and defy the law of its nature up to a certain point.  After that, something goes to smash.  Those are facts at the North Pole, and at the South Pole, and everywhere in between.  Similarly, one can take this race-wide play-instinct, and guide it according to its own law of development to the building up of body and soul far above the danger-line of human ruin. Also, one can suppress it with impunity—for a certain length of time. But like the air, it has to go somewhere ; and if it cannot go the safe way, it will take some other : the energy which creates it must be expressed. To this crude young need with no adequate outlet all sorts of illicit adventures proffer their irresistible lure—petty thefts, trials of brute strength, the aping of older folk in obscene talk and vicious deeds, "crap-playing" in the streets, the smoking of cigarettes, surreptitious drinking, the stealing of older people's "dope."

We understand here in the South, those of us who are somewhat interested in such matters, that these are proven facts concerning the gangs of young toughs in Northern slums. It is perfectly reasonable to quite a number of us that a baseball ground and a boys' club, or an organization of Boy Scouts, will transform a crowd of budding white criminals into decent young humans who delight to obey the law and to require their companions to do likewise : but it does not seem to occur to us, as yet, that this law of the gang is operative except where humanity has a white skin. So instead of buying playgrounds for our poor with our taxes, and furnishing trained directors of play for them, we take many times the sum needed for this simple provision for a normal need, and build great court-houses with it, filled with expensive machinery, human and other, of what we are pleased to call justice ; and put up endless local jails, every one of which is guaranteed, by every law of spiritual dynamics, to poison the folk put into it, and to smother their impulses towards a better life. And then we sit down and commiserate ourselves for being burdened with a people so bent by nature towards crime.

In the summer of 1912, in a Southern city, afternoon playgrounds for Negro children were opened by the combined efforts of a few people of both races.  Negro women of force and ability were engaged to supervise them, and the whole venture was under the direction of a Southern white woman, a graduate of her own state university and of Columbia. The children gathered in the playgrounds like flies.  None of them knew how to play, but they were still plastic with childhood, and responded as childhood everywhere does from the North Pole to the South.  But older children came too—gangs of adolescent boys whose only idea of "fun" was to torment folk weaker than themselves, and to smash

up whatever afforded others pleasure. They
were a whole battalion of thorns in the flesh
all summer long. The white women concerned, having exhausted their own resources, appealed to the local Y. M. C. A.,
and to the pastors of several of the churches,
for a white man who would take the gang in
charge and organize its members as a constructive force in their community. But
though the Y. M. C. A. director and the
pastors tried diligently to find a man to undertake the task, nobody was forthcoming;
and the group continues its boisterous career
towards the chain-gang, where so many of us
believe Negroes gravitate by their own nature rather than by our neglect.

But children are only the beginning of the
story. The play instinct is not an evanes-
cent appurtenance of childhood: it is deep
down among the primal needs of life, as real
and as persistent as the need for air or food.
We educated white people are perfectly
aware of our own need for recreation. We
turn to the woods and the mountains, to golf
and tennis, fishing and camping, whenever
we can possibly afford it, and just as long as
we live. In between whiles we go to the
theatre and the " movies," to baseball and
football games, to the parks, on motoring

trips—any and everywhere that promises us a break in the monotony of life, a bit of relaxation, a little laughter. We begin to understand that the need of these things is bedded so deep in the nature of white people that wage earners are actually more profitable to their employers, in dollars and cents, if they get their bit of vacation in summer time. It has long been customary in the North, and grows yearly more common with us, to give clerks and salespeople two-weeks' playtime a year, with pay; to close department stores at noon on Saturdays in summer ; to let everybody off on holidays. We are learning to do it not simply because we want other people to enjoy themselves, but because our enlightened selfishness is becoming convinced that a workman who never plays can never do the most efficient work.

But it has not occurred to us that natural laws have no special editions for skins of different colours. There are, of course, as many kinds of pleasure as there are individual natures ; and some of them require not only certain temperaments, but certain stages of intellectual advancement, for their enjoyment. No one would claim that a slum Negro could be interested for a moment in much that would give a cultivated white man the keenest pleasure.  But a need common to all humanity has somewhere an answer suited to each man's stage of development ; an answer clean, healthful, and life-giving : and they who withhold it do so to their own peril as well as to the injury of him who needs.

The poor of every nation need play more than any other class, and are more injured by the lack of it.  What else drives New York's wage-earning girls, by scores of thousands, to the low dance-halls of commercialized pleasure ?  They would rather go to decent places, as is shown by the way they crowd the few which are provided : but recreation they must have, or snap under the daily strain of work.  Young men flock to the same places, decent fellows to begin with, often, pitifully eager to meet "some nice girl."   But the associations are too much for their unguarded youth.  It is the exhilaration of the liquor they drink which lures them, not its taste.  They want that glorious sense of freedom which is its first effect, that power to rise in a tumult of life and energy above all that cramps them in their sordid daily lives.  It is the excitement of gambling that draws them—the ecstasy of bated breath, of pulses that throb and thrill.  They never intend to wreck their lives ; only to bring into their poor dull colourlessness a little of sheen and glamour and fire. The lower they are in the economic and the moral scale, in every city of every land, the bleaker and duller their empty lives, the more fiercely this need drives them. A man with a few of the comforts of life, a few inward resources —only a few—may walk without pleasure, maimed indeed, but in a straight path, to the end. But he who has nothing, within or without, neither resource nor help, what shall he do, with only his blank, dead life of drudgery, and his fierce human need for a little joy?

It is so simple it breaks one's heart. Such utter wreckage, such ruin and waste and degradation, such lapsing of men into beastliness—and all for lack of a thing like this, a simple human answer to a vital human need!

Sometimes when I think about us—us Southern white folks—I don't know whether to laugh or to cry. We are good people. I've associated with us all my life, and I know that is true. Ideals stir us as nothing else does. If there is anything Southern people will do it is to spend themselves for an idea— once they catch it. We caught the temperance idea years ago—it is really the germ of our late-developing social consciousness

—and we have fought for it as no other section of America has. Somehow, by the blessing of Providence, our preachers got hold of it by its individually religious end, and many of them have not thought of it as "social service" to this day. So they welcomed it to the fold of orthodoxy, and went forth to fight for it with never a Christian to say them nay, or to suggest that social service was no concern of a church dedicated to the preaching of "the pure gospel." As for results, a look at the wet-and-dry map of the United States in this present year of grace will show that the South is the cleanest part of the map. We do things just that way.

But like other grown-ups, we are mightily like children. A child will clean up his playthings in a whirl of enthusiasm over helping his mother ; and when she comes in, by invitation, to admire the results, she will find the rubbish not cleaned up, but tucked out of sight, and perhaps ruining some of her most cherished finery in its novel seclusion. Only the obvious middle of the room is in order. We have gone at the drink habit just that way.

The Negro's propensity for drink does trouble us. That is one thing about his condition we are aware of. We even feel the menace to the community which drunken Negroes furnish ; and we deplore a development still so low, after all these years of civilization. Nothing, we say, will eradicate the Negro's love of liquor. (We do not specify what we have tried as an eradicator; but whatever it was, it hasn't worked.)

According to our lights, however, and in all sincerity, we have done our duty. We have passed local-option and prohibition laws. We have made a *fiat* sweep of the whole miserable liquor business, with a view, largely, to removing from the play-hours of our very poor, both white and black, one of their three great resources, which are, for both colours in this poorest class, gambling, immorality and drink. But what we have taken with one hand we have given with the other : not something clean to take the place of the unclean ; but the same uncleanness with the added smirch of lawlessness. In all our cities men, nearly all of whom are white, are allowed to open " near-beer " saloons for the open selling of every known intoxicant, and to make a living from the degradation of our poor, both white and black, with the consent and protection of the authorities. When the poor, who are mostly black, go as the drink drives them, we dive into our pockets for more taxes to build larger court-houses and jails; and the women, whom the prisoners might have supported if they had had a better chance to stay sober, are left to choose between the streets for themselves, or work for themselves and the streets for their children. And so the manufacture of criminals, one of our most stupendous industries, and certainly our most expensive luxury, goes bravely on.

Prohibition is good as far as it goes, even though in our cities it does not go at all. But it will never, by itself, do very much more than just slick life up on the outside. It is a purely negative measure, a gigantic Thou shalt not. It has its place in positive life, as many other negations have : but a negation can never construct anything ; its utmost is to clear the ground for construction. And if those who clear the ground construct nothing, somebody else will. Human life, being part of nature, tolerates no vacuum. Temperance measures, to be effective, must be constructive : they must offer something to take the place of what they have driven out. Until the human craving for relaxation, for exaltation of both body and spirit, be cleanly met, it will spend itself on the un-

clean.    And out of uncleanness will come
waste and wreckage, for present and future
generations.

What is there in the South that offers clean
amusement, clean play, to Negroes young or
old? In a recent investigation made by an
International Y. M. C. A. Secretary, himself a
Southern man, four cities were found having
public parks for Negroes.    Four public parks
for Negroes in fifteen Southern states !    Out of
seventeen cities eight reported having picture
shows for Negroes, and nine none.    Of the
picture shows reported half were " very low
and degrading, with the vilest vaudeville
attachments."    In five cities there are theatres
for Negroes—character not specified ; and in
several they are allowed in the peanut gallery
of white theatres ; but the investigator reports
" the better class of Negroes say they will not
go unless for some special attraction, as they
are put with the lowest class of whites."    The
report further declares that the " principal
places of amusement for the male population
[Negro] are the saloons, pool and billiard
rooms."    The saloon people are the quickest
of all whites to recognize the Negro's humanity.    They see that Negroes become
slaves of drink exactly as white men do, and
spend their last nickel for it in the same

manner. In my own city the very large majority of cases in the recorder's court are Negroes, and nearly all their infractions of law are the results of drinking. The city is in a prohibition state. It contains eighty officially licensed near-beer saloons, and seventy-nine of them are run by white men. In practically every city of the South we white people set this object lesson regarding respect for law before the Negroes, and then deplore and despise the innate lawlessness of the black man's nature.

But if diversions other than drinking and lewdness are hard for adult Negroes to come by, what is done for the children? Louisville has two or three playgrounds for them, not very well equipped, but under the direction of the City Park Commissioner, as are the far ampler playgrounds for white children; and New Orleans has recently opened one with semi-official recognition. So far as I can learn these are the only cities in the South which have officially recognized this basal human need as common to white and black. A prominent church and club woman of Nashville gave a playground to Negro children in that city a few years ago; and whites and blacks together have now for two summers provided vacation playgrounds for

Negro children in Augusta, Ga.   That completes the list to date.

Laying aside all altruistic motives, turning our backs on Christ's doctrine of human brotherhood, and acting solely from the standpoint of enlightened selfishness, it would pay the South, just in money, to put a three-acre playground next door to every schoolhouse for both whites and blacks, and to add to the teaching force a director of play for each county, under whose supervision the teachers of the various schools could in turn assume charge of the playground after school hours.   Folk dances would take the place of games with the older children.   We could call them folk games if some of our church people looked askance at the other word.   If the universal enjoyment of movement in rhythmical time could be met in this clean and wholesome fashion it would do more to undermine "animal dancing" than any well-deserved philippic that could be hurled against it.   The best way to get rid of an unclean thing is to put in its place a clean one which meets the need.

The schoolhouse should be the recreation centre for young and old.   For years great corporations have been employing "social engineers" to work among their employees as a matter of sound business policy, to bring up the efficiency of the human end of the machine. A large part of the engineer's duty has lain in providing clean and interesting recreation for folk deadened by drudgery. Lately a city or two has taken the matter up and appointed a city Superintendent of Public Recreation, just as they have a Park Commissioner. There is no sentiment in such an act—no sentimentality, at least. Hard-headed business men have done it, and communities stand to it, and pay the necessary taxes to finance it, because it will pay in human character and happiness, and, in the long run, in dollars as well. So here and yonder, in the most unexpected places, it keeps cropping out in life that what we call Christian doctrines are not doctrines at all. They are laws of human life, and Christ's, not in the sense that He made them up, but in the sense that He understood them and put them into words. When we provide for the human needs of the weakest, we come not upon sacrifice, but on more abundant life for all. For we really are brethren, all of us, and the satisfied need of those who lack is the strength and prosperity of all.

# V

## HUMAN WRECKAGE

**B**UT what of the wreckage already achieved ? What of that fragment of the world-wide ruin most in evidence to our consciousness—the criminals, young and old, of both races, who fill our Southern jails, and work in all possible publicity of disgrace, chained and striped, upon our streets ?

For thousands of years the world has had two theories only about the relation of the state to crime. One is the theory of vengeance, originally the right of the individual, but as civilization progressed a right which became vested in the community. Among Christian nations Moses has been set forth as the champion of this theory ; and " an eye for an eye, a tooth for a tooth " is still widely quoted in justification of this outworn delusion, upon which the criminal law of the nations is founded.

It was doubtless a benevolent law in Moses' day which restricted vengeance, not to the limit of the avenger's power, but to that rough justice which measured the penalty by the offense.  So far as we can decipher those old records, and those of far later generations, to inject into vengeance an idea of justice was not the least of the great lawgiver's achievements.  Many, however, who quote Moses with gusto seem unacquainted with later Biblical literature, in which the exercise of vengeance is distinctly declared to be beyond the province of mankind.

Nevertheless, men cherish it to this day as a sacred and inalienable right.  And lest vengeance unadorned should be insufficient, they have embroidered this first theory with the second—that punishments severe and ingenious beyond what vengeance might demand would act as deterrents to criminals *in posse*.  On this altar of public benevolence the criminal *in esse* is still offered up, a useless and frightful sacrifice to the blindness and folly of men.  It is true the law no longer condemns him to be broken on the wheel, nor burned with faggots of green wood, nor tortured in many of the thousand ways which make the prison history of the past such black reading.

But notwithstanding the rise and spread of a modern penology which is already profoundly influencing criminal procedure in many countries, the vast bulk of the world's criminals are still dealt with under a combination of these two theories. The criminal is punished because punishment is his desert and the state's right ; and his degree of punishment must be severe enough to frighten anybody else from attempting a similar crime. That severity of sentence does not deter others from crime is proven by the criminal history of many centuries, and has long been openly acknowledged by authorities on crime in all countries. It is out of this self-confessed breakdown of the old system that the rise of a new one has become possible.

The foundation of the new system is, in the words of the eminent chairman of the English Prison Commission, " the accepted axiom of modern penology that a prisoner has reversionary rights in humanity." It regards a man convicted of crime not primarily as a criminal, but as an individual who, " by the application of influences or discipline, labour, education, moral and religious, backed up on discharge by a well-organized system of [oversight] is capable of reinstatement into civic life." It flatly denies the Italian theory of " a criminal type," pronouncing it a superstition, pure and simple. It offers abundant evidence that the criminal disposition is produced, largely in individuals physically or mentally weak, by social conditions which have forced their lives along lines of least resistance. It stands for the reformatory, for the indeterminate sentence, release on parole, the permanent separation of prisoners into groups according to type and criminal development, for education, moral, religious and industrial, for labour in outdoor life as far as practicable, for the abolition of prison stripes, and everything calculated to break down self-respect, and for life-detention of all who cannot be restored to society in safety to the community and to themselves.

Twenty-two nations were officially represented in the last International Prison Congress, which met in Washington City three years ago ; three additional governments, Spain, the Transvaal, and Egypt, signified their desire to join ; and negotiations were opened with the governments of China and Japan which indicate that at the next Congress representatives of those governments will take their place in the body as members, instead of taking part unofficially, as heretofore. The members of this Congress differed, as might be supposed, on many points : but they stood as a body for the principles of

the new penology above stated. They also
endorsed the principle that payment should
be allowed the prisoner by the state for his
work over and above the sum necessary for
his own support; and that this remainder
should be turned over to the prisoner's family
if in need.

A point of deepest significance to Americans, North and South, was the unanimous
conviction of all the delegates, home and
foreign, that American local jails were the
worst known to civilization. The United
States government placed a special train at
the disposal of the foreign delegates, and
acted as their host during a tour of investigation which covered most of the country's
great reformatories, adult and juvenile, and
many local jails. It is said that the Tombs,
in New York City, reduced the foreigners to
speechlessness. One of the most eminent
said afterwards that the only thing to do
with it was to tear it down; but the others
found words incompatible with the minimum
of politeness necessary in the presence of a
host. The secretary of the Howard Association of London, when asked, did not hesitate to say that every jail he saw in America
" ought to be wiped off the face of the earth,"
and that "nowhere in Europe do such con-

HOME OF ATLANTA NEGRO WHO WAS HIS OWN ARCHITECT AND BUILDER.

156B

ditions exist." The newly-elected president of the Congress, Sir Evelyn Ruggles-Brise, in extending an invitation for the next meeting to be held in England, begged the Americans "out of their humanity" to consider the case of "the thousands of petty offenders now passing through your city and county jails in such appalling numbers."

The reformatories of a few of the Northern states confessedly lead the world, and the principles of human restoration which they have demonstrated are spreading to the states of the West; but we of the South lag behind in every phase of reformatory and preventive work. The only point at which we are strictly up with the procession is in the matter of our local jails. They are like those of the rest of America, well adapted to the one specific end of manufacturing criminals out of that vast company of petty offenders not yet beyond the pale of citizenship.

I was talking with a friend not long ago about a certain local jail. A white woman who had once worked for her had been arrested on some charge, and had appealed to her for help. She had gone to the jail with a lawyer, a friend of hers, but had been refused permission to see the prisoner. The lawyer had been passed in at once, but the jailer stopped my friend.

"No, ma'am," he declared with respectful positiveness ; "you can't go in there. It ain't no place for a lady to be in, nor to see. It ain't fit."

"And he had a white woman in there!" exclaimed my friend ; "a white woman, in a place unfit for a lady even to see! I told him if she could stand staying in it I could stand seeing it, but he wouldn't let me in."

I sympathized with her indignation : but was it any better for a black woman than for a white one ? The white woman should have had a little better chance than the other to resist the moral contagion of the place, and should have been less of a menace to the community when she came out. But the Negroes, and many, too, of the whites, if they ever had a chance before the law grips them, lose it in the jail the law provides ; lose it before they are even proven guilty of the crime with which they are charged. Men grown old in crime and debauchery are, in nearly all our jails, thrown with first offenders, often with mere boys. The accommodations provided for unconvicted American citizens violate the laws of decency and health in regard to the commonest physical needs.

There is no privacy, no cleanliness. Everything in his surroundings combines to brand on the offender's consciousness the fact that he is no longer regarded as a being with human rights, reversionary or otherwise. His relation to life is purely that of the committer of a crime.

He may be just a boy, his offense a trifle; or, if more serious, the outcome, not of premeditated wickedness, but of a thwarted love of adventure, youth's natural flare of high spirits turned awry. In some of our cities such an offender would get what he needs— separate confinement beforehand, and an investigation, rather than a trial before a specially constituted court. A real effort would be made to understand not what the boy did, but why he did it; and after being dealt with by the judge on that line chiefly, he would be turned over to a probation officer whose duty it would be to watch over him, and assist him to moral convalescence. The law should give the judge, as it does in Denver, certain powers to enforce, if necessary, parental cooperation in helping the boy, and in correcting wrong home conditions. With the right kind of judges and probation officers a vast deal of human wreckage is prevented by these courts.

But we have few of them in the South : and there is little of the kind of care needed given to young Negro delinquents.    In what I am told is one of the best-managed juvenile courts of the South the probation officers for the Negro children are Negro women.    That is an immense improvement on the old chain-gang way, of course; but adolescent boys, white or black, will not be very profoundly influenced by anything or anybody feminine. They need a man, and a wise one.

In only a few places, however, does the matter of probation come up.    For the majority of our lawbreakers, young and old, one sure destination waits—the chain-gang, sometimes more euphemistically known as the convict camp.    Here prisoners of all degrees of criminality are thrown promiscuously together, and clothed in stripes to advertise them to all beholders as outlaws from the human family.    They wear individual chains in the daytime, which are fastened together at night.    And they endure whatever of suffering, degradation, insult and injustice their individual keepers choose to bestow upon them.

A Southern Bishop, living in one of our largest cities, recently had a visit from a white man in a dirty, frowsy, unkempt suit, who announced himself as a convict discharged forty-eight hours before from the coal mines near by, which are worked by convict labour. Being questioned, he admitted that he had eaten but twice since his discharge. A Negro had given him some corn bread the first day, and a barkeeper on the next had given him a sandwich and a drink of whiskey. He refused the food and money the Bishop offered him. He had come, he said, to tell the story of what was done to the prisoners in those mines ; he had promised the other convicts before he left that he would carry the story to some Christian, and see if he would take the matter up. If he took anything for himself, he said, it might cast suspicion on his tale.

He was a well-educated man. He said he had been an editor. A wrong had been done to a member of his family ; in a blaze of anger he had shot and killed the offender; and he had been sentenced to three years at hard labour, which he had served.

The men were worked in gangs, under convict foremen, and each gang was assessed so many tons per day. If they mined more they were credited with the excess, to be paid for it when they left the camp. All credits, however, were given by the foremen, themselves convicts ; and they could, and did, give the credits, not to those who earned them, but to those who shared with their overseers, or bribed them in other ways. The foremen carried 'horrible whips ; and they used them constantly, unmercifully, without warning and without provocation. Men were beaten and kicked and injured until it was not at all an unknown thing, the convict said, for a man to put his left hand on the train rail and let the coal car run over it and crush it off. Then he had to be sent to some other camp, being useless for mining. It might be just as bad, of course ; but there was always a chance. This convict had stuck it out. He had been told that he had no overtime pay coming to him. He had received the clothes he wore, taken from some newly-entered convict, instead of the new suit required by law, and had been turned out, penniless, to go back to the world in newness of life, and conduct himself in such an irreproachable manner, after the lesson he had had, as not to get into a convict camp again.

The Bishop told his story quietly, as his habit is, while we sat gasping.

" What did you *do ?* " we demanded.

" I made him take a little money, for one thing—as a loan. He wouldn't take much :

but I followed him down the street and begged till he had to take a little. And I talked to some men who have influence. There is a public meeting called for the seventeenth. There will be men from all over the state, and I think the matter will be probed to the bottom. We may get our state laws reformed before we get through."

But one state is not enough. In my own state, which is not the one of the Bishop's convict, the leaders of the Men and Religion Movement in our capital city have published a list of the barbarities of our convict camps which sound like the Middle Ages. Twenty years ago, in the same state, an investigator appointed by the Governor reported exactly the same conditions. And these states are not behind some of the others. Four of our states, however—Kentucky, Missouri, Tennessee and Texas—are in the honour list of twenty-one states which have adopted the indeterminate sentence and the parole law ; yet three of these retain the convict lease or convict labour system. In a few states the Governor has power to restore citizenship to a discharged convict. But in Texas, Kentucky and Tennessee no man convicted of crime remains an outlaw except by his own will. Citizenship is restored by law to every convicted criminal who, after due testing when released on parole, proves worthy of that trust. The last taint of his sin is cast behind him by the law, and he takes his place again, a man among men. "As far as the east is from the west ——." Isn't that the normal way, the way that *works* because men are made to respond to it?

I was waiting at a railroad station not long ago when a frightened-looking Negro boy of about eighteen came by in the custody of three big policemen, who stood guard about him till the patrol wagon appeared and swallowed him up. After the crowd dispersed I learned from one of the policemen that the boy had been caught in the act of stealing a box of cigars. The policeman thought he would get fifteen years for it; but seeing my horror, and wishing, evidently, to oblige a lady if possible, he reconsidered the matter and said maybe he would get off with ten years, seeing he was not really grown. I remembered the boy who was sentenced to three years for taking eleven dollars and forty-six cents : but that judge had especially pointed out that the sentence was unusually merciful. This boy's judge might well give him ten years of enforced criminal association for his theft : there was no telling.

I remembered another time, some years ago, when I was waiting for another train, at a junction in the mountains of a Southern state. The county sheriff was waiting also, with two white boys of seventeen or eighteen, moonshiners. The boys were chained together by their wrists and by their necks, with what looked like trace-chains. The sheriff had evidently imbibed their whiskey, probably for safe-keeping. He swaggered about, a coarse, not ill-tempered man, a pistol protruding from either pocket of his coat. He talked loudly, joking the boys about their capture and the becomingness of their present adornments. They tried hard to imitate his manner, and to wear an air of jaunty and amused indifference ; but their eyes were frightened and ashamed.

Oh, the folly of it ! The blind, stupid, brutal *uselessness* of it, the wicked waste of human lives and souls !

What had any of these boys, white or black, done, in their isolation, their ignorance, their stunted moral growth, unfriended, untaught—what had they done which gave society the right to seize their poor, starved lives and break and poison them in its foul prisons beyond hope of recovery for all time ? Even if we had the right, what good does it do? The veriest madman out of Bedlam would hardly claim that our convict camps benefit the prisoners : but do they deter others from crime?

The census of the United States can answer that question ; and the prison records of all civilized countries will join with the penologists of the world in confirming what the census says. Every year a vast number of arrests are made, and a less vast number of prisoners are discharged. *Less* vast. Each year our prison population receives an added permanent deposit from this great stream of human misery and ignorance and sin, as it washes through those black and awful places where men already injured are permanently deformed. Such measures have never lessened crime : they provoke it always, everywhere, since prisons were. The more cruelly or publicly a crime is punished the more surely it drives suggestion home to some ill-balanced nature, and rouses it to imitation. The punishment seems to add the last irresistible attraction to those on the border of criminality.

So far from stopping crime, our present system, with its public and private humiliations of the offender, propagates crime in both the criminal and the beholder. Whatever beats down a prisoner's remnants of self-respect is a blow not only at his manhood, but at the manhood of the state. Our prisons are great spawning-beds, where the crime of the community is gathered in that the crime of the state may pass over it and fructify it, sending out swarms of new evil influences to squirm and twist and spread in all the ooze and slime of the community, that our criminal supply may never fail.

We need more rational methods in our whole criminal procedure. When one has scarlet fever or diphtheria one is quarantined, not for a specified time, but until one can be safely restored to community life, as shown by one's personal condition. The criminal must also be treated as an individual. Something must be learned of his heredity, his environment, the causes which led to his crime. Only so may one attempt his restoration. To expect to attain it on any other basis than the one of sympathetic understanding is as unreasonable as to expect one course of treatment to cure every form of disease. Even the same disease requires different treatment for different cases; and to fix the term of a man's imprisonment by the crime he has committed is to ignore the dominating factor in the case—his personality.    His personality, not his past offense, makes him a social menace.    He should be imprisoned as long, and only as long, as his personality threatens danger to the community.

Dean Kirchwey, of the Faculty of Law of Columbia University, in a great address on " Ending the Reign of Terror " said :

" A demonstration of the fact, which we may well consider indubitable, that criminal conduct is usually, if not always, the result of conditions more or less beyond the control of the delinquent, cannot fail to shake the theory of moral responsibility upon which the vindictive idea of punishment is based, as well as to allay and in time overcome the feeling of resentment which such conduct now excites.    And, on the other hand, a study of the psychology of the mob, and of the reaction of the existing penal system on the moral sense of the community will show how far it is safe to go in mitigating the rigours of the criminal law in a given jurisdiction  .   .   . [until] such time as may be required to bring the community to a better appreciation of the nature of crime, and the conditions which determine it.   .   .   .

" The doctrine that punishment is inflicted on the offender as a warning to others has

come to be the orthodox view.   .   .   .   There
is something touching in the unquestioning
faith of the legal profession and of the man
in the street in the efficacy of this vicarious
suffering for crimes not yet committed.   Yet
it remains a matter of faith as yet unsupported
by evidence.   .   .   .

"The fact that a very large proportion—in
some countries more than fifty per cent.—of
criminals under confinement have previously
undergone prison punishment seems to indicate that as a deterrent punishment by
imprisonment leaves something to be desired.   .   .   .

"The principle that punishment may
.   .   .   without reformatory influences be a
means of moral amendment finds expression
in many judicial utterances.   It is obviously
a well-meant, but mistaken attempt to bring
the sanctions of the moral law and of the
ecclesiastical dispensation to the aid of the
criminal law.   .   .   .   This imputes to the
law a sanctity which the criminal would be
the last to concede to it ; and so quite apart
from the vile and degrading conditions under
which this work of grace was to be effected,
it is not to be wondered at that we find no
traces of its efficacy.   .   .   .

"The principle of the reformation of criminals during imprisonment  .  .  .  does not assume that all criminals are capable of reformation, or even of improvement, nor that those who are can all be brought up to the level of good citizenship. It does assume, however, that most men and women, and all children, will respond to the steady pressure of a wholesome, uplifting environment  .  .  . and it has already proven its faith by its works.  .  .  . It must have cognizance of the life history of every individual committed to prison, with his heredity and environment. It studies him in prison—his needs, his capacities, his aspirations, his mental and moral equipment, his health, his reaction to  .  .  . prison life. It follows him after his discharge.  .  .  . It levies on all the sciences that deal with man—law, medicine, criminology, sociology.  .  .  .

"The next few years will give us new data of great importance.  .  .  . But there will be no facts for him who regards the criminal law as an instrument for venting wrath and hate on a fallen—and convicted—brother ; none for him who would keep his fellow man in subjection to his iron law by terror ; none for him who would work redemption through another's suffering.  .  .  . The new moral atmosphere which has made every man his brother's keeper will be felt in the law courts as well as in the home and street. The new attitude of the state towards children of tender years will soon mark her attitude towards her erring children of a larger growth."

Those of us who can find comfort in a fact so painful may be assured that we of the South are not alone in the possession of a prison system outworn and barbarous. Nothing in our awful camps could be worse than what has been found, in most recent years, in the state prisons of several of the richest and most enlightened states of the North and West ; and if they were all investigated the present black list would doubtless be longer than it is. But this fact concerns us only as it shows that our own conditions are part of a world-wide horror, which the best thought of the world has set itself to destroy. The reformation of our whole prison system is our part of a world-task.

We need a Southern Prison Commission, appointed by the governors of the states, not to revise our prison system, but to study conditions, here and elsewhere, and to formulate a new system abreast of modern experience, and founded on bed-rock truth and justice, instead of on the philosophy of the Middle Ages. The members of the Commission should be men of broad humanity and of strong common sense. Such men could, by the authority of their respective governors, make individual and unannounced visits, each to a number of prisons in his own state. Then they could examine the best the world can show them; the Denver juvenile court; the Colorado state farm, where "hardened" criminals are turned into men, without stripes, threats, chains or armed guards; the District of Columbia prison farm; the wonderful work for women at Bedford, N. Y., for men at Great Meadow, and for children at Industry, in the same state; the Kansas City municipal farm, a new idea in local government; the Massachusetts farms for vagrants and inebriates, and many more.

This Commission would find at least three points in the South where Negro lawbreakers are being successfully trained towards good citizenship. In Virginia it is being done at the suggestion, and under the supervision, of a state officer, and with the backing of the legislature. In Georgia and Alabama it is being done by unknown and unlettered Negroes, whose loving hearts have led them into a wisdom not to be attained by any amount of unloving knowledge.

The State Superintendent of Charities and

Correction in Virginia, a large-hearted, broad-minded man, fully abreast of the developments of modern penology, has, in the last three years, taken from the Richmond penitentiary one hundred and fifty convicted Negro "criminals," all under fifteen years of age, and has placed them, under proper supervision, in good Negro homes, as members of the respective families. He tells me one hundred and forty-three of these boys are "making good." They are growing up into self-respecting and wealth-producing citizens, instead of becoming a recurring charge upon the state, which is the usual result of our ordinary methods of dealing with Negro first offenders.

At Ralph, Ala., is the Sam Daily reformatory, still called by his name, though Sam Daily himself has made his humble exit from life with no trumpets to proclaim him a hero, unless the angels sounded them on the other side. He was a full-blooded Negro, with no touch of efficiency as the gift of another race.

A white Alabamian, a city judge, moved with compassion for the young Negro delinquents brought before him, called for some good Negro of like compassion to give the boys a chance. Sam Daily responded, donating himself, his family, and one hundred and twenty-five acres of land to their use. First and last he took about three hundred boys from the Birmingham juvenile court, paid their way to the railroad station nearest his farm, fed them, clothed them, taught them industry, cleanliness and honour. I am told that ninety-five per cent. of his boys " make good."

The most curious thing about this enterprise is the fact that this poor Negro, who was never able to finish paying for his own farm, spent years of his life converting lawbreakers from a public liability to a public asset without receiving any public money to help bear the expenses of the process. Individual white men have helped him, and now help his widow, by making up deficits when they occur ; but there is no regular public appropriation for this great and public service. The Southern Presbyterian Church, however, now pays regularly the salary of a trained Negro assistant at the reformatory. A white man, formerly a large slave-owner, who knows the reformatory well, writes me, in regard to its success with the boys, " I should call this forlorn effort to help the helpless a modern miracle." Only it isn't a miracle : it is natural law given a chance to work.

The third of these demonstrations of the response of Negro delinquents to good influences is made at the Paul Moss Orphanage at Augusta, Ga. Paul Moss is a Negro of rather limited education who gave up an excellent income as a skilled mechanic to devote his life to aiding Negro waifs and juvenile delinquents. He put all his savings into a small farm, where he has supported his charges with a little help from a few whites of the city and one or two Northern visitors. He is able to give the boys not much book education, but teaches them practical religion and a few trades. In the last six years he has sent out one hundred and sixty boys, half of whom were from the city juvenile court, the others being orphans and waifs in process of becoming delinquents. One hundred and fifty of these boys are " making good."

Each of these separate experiments shows that the response made by Negro delinquents to a helpful and sympathetic environment equals that made by the same class of other races—about ninety-five per cent. Would not our Southern Prison Commission consider this method of dealing with lawbreakers economically superior to the one now in general use? Even where we have reformatories for young Negroes under state or county supervision the inmates are treated as prisoners, dressed in some kind of distinctive, branding uniform, kept under lock and key —and eventually landed, very many of them, in our prisons and convict camps. And we think that fact is explained by the Negro's criminal tendencies. The Commission, with all the evidence before it, might decide differently.

The Commission would look into the evils of convict labour as employed in many "model" prisons, so called, where men are driven beyond the limit of health under a contract system as vicious as our own, and turned out after years of alleged industrial training skilled only in some occupation employment in which is impossible outside of prison walls. They would go thoroughly into the question of the state's right, while attempting to restore a man to normal citizenship, to forbid his performance of the primal human duty to contribute to the support of his own family ; and would examine the methods by which innocent women and children are beginning to be saved from this usual and unjust punishment.

They would learn what public services prisoners perform elsewhere, while being at the same time restored to manhood. We are too much in the habit of looking at the thing done, and ignoring the man who does it. Many of us feel, for instance, that in setting her convicts to work on the public roads—a most beneficent public service—one of our states has taken front rank in the treatment of her criminals. Yet that state clothes those men in stripes, as we all do, and works them in chains, on the public roads, under armed guards destitute of knowledge or fitness in the fine art of saving human wreckage.

In New Zealand in the last decade the convicts have planted 20,000,000 trees for the state, timbering waste lands, *and reclaiming the men*. But they do not wear stripes in New Zealand. The idea there is to deliver them from past degradation, not to sear it in for present and future injury. Denmark reforests her waste lands with men who, like the land, are in process of restoration. Prussia and Switzerland employ them to care for the great state forests : and they are employed in a number of our own Western states in various works of reclamation, though too often, with us, the uppermost idea is the reclamation, not of men, but of property.

All these things our Southern Prison Commission would consider ; and far above the great and profitable work of reclaiming and enriching the wide waste lands of the South by prison labour, they would set that greater and more profitable work of preventing the wide waste of human life, and reclaiming that already in process of ruin.

A prison system suited to human needs—the needs of prisoners, of their families, of the community at large—could be formulated, and presented to all our states, together with the information necessary, and with the weight of this South-wide Commission behind it.    In principle, if not in all its details, it would be adopted in some states ; and ultimately in all, as the experience of the foremost illuminated the wisdom of its provisions.

We need no revision of what we now have : we need a new penology, based on a conception of human life radically opposed to most that underlies our theory of punishment to-day.

We need to take up the call already being heard throughout the civilized world—a call for *trained* men and women to create the new profession of Healers-of-men-in-prison.    We would not, even in our politics-fuddled cities put fifteenth century " leeches " (if we could get them) in charge of our public hospitals. Yet we count any ignorance competent to take unlimited control of sick souls and abnormal minds. In the recent Prison Congress America and Hungary joined hands to express the conviction of the penologists of the world that this professional training of prison officers—men already fitted by nature for such difficult and important work—was a vital need in the progress of humanity towards a sane and successful treatment of the world-problem of human wreckage.

## VI

## SERVICE AND COÖPERATION

IF I were asked what the mass of the
Negroes most need that we should give
them, I think only one answer could be
given which would go to the root of the whole
matter.  And that deepest need is not at all
a Negro need, but a human one : we ourselves,
as a people, share it profoundly.

They need ideals.  The lives of so many
of them seem just a chaos of wants, so that
one stands at first dumb with bewilderment :
so many fundamental needs, so much emptiness where there must be solid foundations if
anything worth while is built up !  But that
which will open a way to fill all these empty
spaces is a vision of something higher in
their own souls ; something higher, yet not
too far or cold to kindle a spark of desire in
their hearts, to quicken them, by vision and
aspiration.

If we will look back over the last fifty years
we will see, perhaps, how little of this foremost essential of human advance we have
furnished for them.  Some things we have

done, I know. We have paid millions for their education in the public schools : but have we cared how it was spent ? The superintendent of education in one of our states, in a recent report, pronounces the Negro public schools of that commonwealth utterly inefficient.

He charges their wretched failure on the white county superintendents, many of whom, he says, never go near the Negro schools under them, nor concern themselves with the selection of fit teachers, nor with their improvement after they are selected. This story would fit more states than one. We could squander ten times the millions already spent in education like that without creating a single impulse towards better things : there is never any vivifying power in indifference.

Yet our public schools for Negroes have done good—a world of it. Some of this must be credited to those among us who have honestly sought the Negro's good. The rest, I think, is due to the Negroes themselves, and to those once-so-hated " Yankees " who first made possible to Negro teachers a suitable preparation for their work.

Love is the world's lifting-force. It is like the light, which yearly lifts untold tons of cold, dead matter to the tree-tops in the beauty of green leaves. When we see leaves we know light has been at work : nothing else could lift matter up there so that leaves could be. And wherever we find a trace of spiritual quickening, a budding of dormant life, however scant, we know by the same token that Love has been at work : there is no other force which produces that effect. The uplift of the Negroes through the public schools, small as it is compared with what it might have been with the same expenditure of money, has chiefly come, not from our sometimes grudging provision, but from ideals kindled in some Negroes' souls by love and sacrifice other than our own.

The Northerners who came down here to teach the Negroes were ignorant of our past, of our conditions, of the underlying causes of our new antagonism to the Negroes—of all the circle of white life which looked to them so inexplicably cruel and wrong. They were only less ignorant about the Negroes, their traditions, their stage of race-growth, their true relation to Southern life. Few people had learned to be world-dwellers then ; and these eager Northern folk, who saw a need and longed to meet it, translated neither white life nor black into world-terms. They made blunders, of course ; and a good many

A RESPECTED NEGRO DOCTOR.

PAINE COLLEGE, AUGUSTA, GA.

182B

Negroes acquired some knowledge at the expense of more wisdom. We have all seen white people do the same thing. And certainly the South never tried to help the situation. So far as explanation or assistance went we maintained a silence which was more than felt, while these from another world came and wrestled with our problems in all good faith, and according to their darkness and their light.

But with all the mistakes and friction, the energy wasted or turned to loss, these people brought one thing with them which is never wholly lost. It may be hindered, partly negatived, robbed of its full fruition by many things: but always love bears fruit. They brought with them that principle of life. They kindled a light in darkened hearts; they sent out thousands of Negroes fired with ideals of service to their race. And they have saved the situation, so far as it has been saved, for our Negro public schools.

We gave the Negroes ideals once. The North is dull of understanding at this point, as we are dull at others. It cannot take in the fact that slavery and ideals could exist contemporaneously. Yet once the North itself, and in the most strenuous days of its New England conscience, was unaware of

any incompatibility between the two. It is
the big brother again, forgetting his own so-
recent ignorance, and ready with paste-pot
and label for the younger child.

The existence of slavery we long accepted
much as we did the weather—as a dispensation of providence which it were idle to inquire into. But we had a genuine affection
for the Negroes, and out of it we met this
need for ideals—an even deeper need than
emancipation from physical slavery. Every
Protestant denomination in the South had its
white missionaries among the slaves, and all
together they had nearly half a million slave
members at the outbreak of the war. One
church alone, the Southern Methodist, spent
nearly two million dollars in missions to the
Negroes prior to 1861, and had over three
hundred white missionaries at work among
them when the war broke out. The individual slave-owners, the very great majority of
whom were Christian people, did even more.
Men and women, they taught their slaves the
Bible—not, as has been ignorantly sug-
gested, to enforce the duties of meekness
and obedience, but because the love of God
in their own hearts necessitated their impart-
ing it to those around them. My own
mother was typical of her class, and no one

who came in contact with her could have imagined that her service to the Negroes was caused by anything but the spirit which transfigured her whole life from day to day. Such women held regular Sunday-schools for their slaves, and often the white children of the household sat with the black ones to learn the Law which was over both of them alike. In times of rejoicing or of trouble the white people went to the Negro homes as friends ; and in sickness they cared for them personally, often with their own hands.

Those among us who deny the Negro's capacity to respond to ideals should remember his faithfulness in time of war and temptation, and the beauty of character which even the most prejudiced of us admit belonged to " the old-time Negro." The admission, coupled, as it usually is, with sweeping charges against the character of the Negro of to-day, is the severest arraignment of Southern Christianity which can be brought against it. And we bring it ourselves, unseeing.

But the truth has had its witnesses, all along. There were women all over the South who, like my mother, went serenely on in the path of love, even during reconstruction days, ministering to the sick and the poor about them, regardless of the colour of their skins, and seeing only needs which love must meet. There were, in every state, men like Governor Colquitt, of Georgia, who as slave-owner, impoverished Confederate, and governor of his state, would tuck his Bible under his arm any afternoon in the week, and go to some Negro cabin, where he would read and teach and pray, talking with the family as friend with friends, advising, comforting and inspiring them.

Nor did the next generation utterly fail. Through all the turmoil of reconstruction some passed the spirit of service to their children.  An Alabama woman, for instance, who was widowed by the war, remained on her remote plantation, where she spent her life teaching the Negroes of the neighbourhood free of charge.  Her daughters took up her work, and carry it on to this day.  I know a brilliant Kentucky woman, daughter of a great slave-owner of that state who was at one time its governor, who has been a helper to Negro church workers, and to any Negro in need, her whole long, beautiful life.  Another friend, a woman of wealth and influence, a leader among the women of the South to-day, taught a Bible class of Negroes for sixteen years, until her strength failed under her accumulating work for the unprivileged.

Space fails for the instances known to even one person.    One more must suffice.

Just after the war a South Carolinian, a graduate of Brown University and a devout Baptist, went to a Georgia city and gathered about him a little knot of Negro boys who wanted to become Baptist preachers.    He taught them there for years, spending himself to give ideals to the ignorant and the poor, cut off from all other association.    For the white people were bitter in those days, and despised him where they did not hate.    It was one man's vision against a city's blindness—that world-old story of ignorance, and of light no darkness can quench.    He is forgotten to-day by all but a few Negroes, one of whom, a fine, strong man who had felt his touch, told me his story.    But the black boys to whom he gave ideals have gone out to give their people light.    Their church is strong in Georgia, and these men lead it. One of them is its chief pastor in my own city ; and so well has he responded to his teacher's efforts that the white people of the town are all his friends.    When he was ill not long ago the daily paper reported his condition, and gave the names of several of the leading business men who went to his home to inquire how he did.

Yet few of the whites who speak of this Negro and of the others who were taught with him, as " the kind all Negroes ought to be" have any idea where the real springs of their lives were found.  Some of us, turning away from the South's long tradition of service to the Negro race, knowing only the disjointed years of bitterness, feel only contempt, or at best a puzzled surprise, that any white Southerner should lower himself by stooping to help a Negro, or should persuade himself that they are worth the effort.

Yet we have never offered them ideals out of a living sympathy that they have not responded, for themselves and for their race. No one who knows the better class of Negroes can fail to be impressed with the spirit of sacrifice and service which is shared by nearly all of them.  They follow that law of human life under which any race, in common stress of any kind, draws closer the band of brotherhood, and lives for the common good.

And oh, we white people are waking up ! The thrill of the North's awaking, long ago begun, and not yet ended, is with me still ; but these are my very own ! Some of us have worked and waited so long.  There have been years when the only warrant for hope was in the long look at the Race of Man, and the Love which leads it on. But that was warrant enough.—And now? Just a few of the signs—a few.

For long our churches have set a standard for us ; and even though they themselves have not lived up to it, the pegs were down, and visible to the careful eye. In 1876 the Southern Presbyterians opened a theological school for Negroes at Tuscaloosa, Ala. For nineteen years the pastor of the white Presbyterian church of the town was also the head of this school, which has had only Southern whites as teachers from the beginning. The yearly income, provided by the denomination, had risen from four hundred dollars the first year to fifteen thousand twenty years later. The theologues pay their board and tuition by working on the school farm under expert teaching. They go out to preach a gospel of love, morality, cleanliness, hard work, and modern methods of farming ; also of friendliness to their white neighbours. I am told, by those who know the section about Tallapoosa, that race relations there are not of the problem kind. There has been response to ideals from both whites and blacks. The present head of the school is the son of a Mississippi slave-owner.

A few years after this school was started the Southern Methodists opened an institution in Augusta, Ga., for the training of Negro preachers, teachers, and other leaders for the race. Its first president was a former slave-owner, who resigned the chair of English in a strong college to take the position at a most problematical salary. It cannot be denied that the school lived "at a poor dying rate" for several years : but the denomination was officially committed to it as a proper work for white Christians to undertake ; Southern white college men and women have officered it from the first ; and for eighteen years the church Board of Education has put its needs before the people, and, in coöperation with its president and faculty, has gradually won for it a better support.

These are, so far as I know, the only schools maintained exclusively by Southern whites for Negroes ; but the Episcopal church has a number of schools for them in which Southern as well as Northern whites teach ; and part of their support, which comes from their General Mission Board, is drawn from the Southern dioceses. The Southern Baptists, who have long made an annual appropriation for the education of Negroes at schools of other churches, are now preparing to open a theological seminary for them.

The first Southern settlement for Negroes is conducted by the son of an Alabama banker and former slaveholder. It is in Louisville, and is of late years jointly financed by the Northern and Southern Presbyterians. This settlement, I am told, is largely responsible for Louisville's Negro playgrounds and probation officers. This city also has a fine public library for Negroes,[1] with a Negro librarian and two assistants, all under the white librarian who is the head of the city system. A children's room is well patronized ; and branches are maintained at some of the public schools. In a private letter the white head of the system declares the Negro library an untold blessing to the race. The use of a room in the building is allowed, free of charge, to clubs and other educational and recreational gatherings. The children, he writes, respond readily to guidance, and are eager for good books. The number of adult patrons grows steadily. The library, which is a beautiful building, was given by Mr. Carnegie, and cost $25,000.00. It is maintained by the city of Louisville. Libraries for

[1] Since this was written a second branch public library for Negroes has been opened in Louisville.

Negroes have also been given by Mr. Carnegie to New Orleans, to Nashville, and to Meridian, Miss., the city authorities guaranteeing ample support.

I can learn of but two other Negro public libraries in the South.    One, at Galveston, is the gift of a citizen of that place, whose will made provision for a library for each race. The librarian said that the children were being helped by it to a large extent.    The response among adults was less marked.    The other public library for Negroes is at Jacksonville, Fla. ; and my last report from it, some time ago, stated that it was not as efficient as it should be, because only a room in a corner of the building for whites was available, so that it was impossible to make efforts to extend the work ; but their present capacity was taxed.

Here is a scarcely-touched opportunity to create ideals for a race.    These Carnegie libraries are among the wisest investments in the South.    But some of us, like the children in the market-place, are hard to please. If the Negroes care nothing for books we say they are stupid and vicious-minded : if one proposes antidoting this dangerous condition with the best literature, sympathetically applied, we cry out against the

Negro's uppishness, and want him taught to work.

He ought to be taught to work, no doubt. The great majority of Negroes, like the majority of every race, must always work with their hands.   There is a deal more of what is called drudgery to be done in the world than of everything else put together ; and most of us have our share of it to perform. But no one to whom work is drudgery has ever been rightly taught to work.   I believe this lack of proper training is at the bottom of nine-tenths—or maybe eleven-tenths—of all the laziness and shiftlessness of the poor which does not come from sub-normal physical conditions.   Drudgery is not work : it is a mental attitude towards work which comes from ignorance or from physical weakness. The narrower the round of a man's life, or a woman's, the more they need outlook and horizon.   The world over, the world's poor have been set to do the hardest work in a perfectly detached, unrelated way, without reasons, without background, without a trace of world-connections ; and they usually find it a very boring job, and shirk it when they can, naturally.

We are learning rapidly to broaden the white worker's horizon through the industrial training given in our public and normal schools, and in our agricultural colleges; and in some of our cities part of this training is given to Negroes, some of it of a high order. In Richmond County, Georgia, this industrial work has been extended by the county itself, with no outside aid, to the Negro country schools. We have there a superintendent who looks closely after the schools of both races; and the county superintendent of industrial training gives as efficient oversight and help to the Negro schools, city and country, as to the white. I speak of this county because, living in it, I happen to know about it. That many others do as well I do not doubt.

But the great impulse towards rational training, towards an education which really educates, in the Negro country schools has come from the Jeanes Fund, given by a Northern woman, and administered by a Southern man, the grandson of a great slaveholder, a scholar and educator of distinction. I know of no other one force in Negro life more beneficent than this. It is demonstrating in every one of our states the kind of work needed in their rural schools, and its quickening influence grows with the years. Virginia, first of all the South, appointed a superintendent of Negro rural public schools, a Phi Beta Kappa College graduate and a man for the South to be proud of. Kentucky, Georgia, North Carolina and Alabama have followed the example; and the other states are bound to do likewise or to see themselves out-distanced in the production of wealth in the not-far-distant future. For it is human nature to love work when ideals are put into it, when it has a background and a horizon.

The Y. M. C. A. is doing, through Southern secretaries, a work which can hardly be estimated. Six thousand students have been enrolled in Y. M. C. A. study classes in Southern colleges to study the Negro and the white man's duty to him. Already various forms of settlement and Sunday-school work have grown out of this study. In fifteen years these young men will be the leaders of the South; and even now the attitude of our colleges and universities, faculties and students, is an appreciable factor in the changing public sentiment.

The Y. M. C. A. has also a large coloured organization. Forty-one associations with over sixty thousand members are enrolled. Here again is a great opportunity to help create ideals for a race. In our cities there is no better way to fight intemperance and many other forms of vice among the Negroes, than to provide them with a good Y. M. C. A. building, and to help them get it fully on its feet.

The women of the Southern Methodist church are the only ones in the South as yet carrying on organized work for Negroes. For over twenty-five years they have been the South's women-pioneers along social service lines, first to whites and now to blacks. They opened the first settlement in the South, employed the first visiting nurse, opened the first free clinic, and introduced free kindergartens and industrial training at many points where they were previously unknown.

Twelve years ago they built two industrial cottages for girls at the church's school for Negroes in Augusta, and have since provided for the industrial training there, besides erecting recently a $25,000.00 dormitory. This sum was raised from several sources. Half of it was given by Southern white women, some of them giving as much as a thousand dollars each ; five thousand was given by the General Education Board ; and the rest was raised by a Negro man from the white Southern Methodist conferences.

In addition to this, these women will

shortly open a farm school for Negro boys in Mississippi, five hundred acres of land having been recently given them by a Southern white man for this purpose.

In 1911 they appointed an Alabama woman, a college graduate, as secretary for Negro work. Her headquarters were located in Augusta, where she has opened the white South's second settlement for Negroes, the one in Louisville being the first.

The Augusta vacation playgrounds, secured by the coöperation of people of both races, are an outcome of this work, which, inadequately housed and provided for as it is, is full of promise and interest. The children, nearly all from the poorest class, are as responsive as—well, as children, the world around : their development, in their various clubs and classes, is as striking as in any children of like class anywhere. The kindergartner is a coloured woman, a graduate of one of the best of the schools established by Northern missionaries after the war, and a power for good among her people.

But however institutions may be built up or multiplied, the South-wide need is a South-wide turning of the hearts of the strong to help the weak both by personal service and by coöperation with capable Negro leaders.

To this need a number of Southern agencies at last begin to address themselves.

The will of the late Miss Caroline Phelps Stokes, a well-known Northern philanthropist, provided for the endowment of fellowships in the state universities of Virginia and Georgia "to enable Southern youth of broad sympathies to make a scientific study of the Negro, and of his adjustment to American civilization." These fellowships were accepted in the spirit of their founder, and in the belief that "any national program looking to the adjustment of relations must be based on a far wider knowledge of actual conditions than we now have." The university of Georgia has just published the results of the investigations made by its first Fellow under this foundation. He is the son of a member of the university faculty, and has spent a year in a close and sympathetic study of the Negroes of Athens, the university town, and of their relations with the whites. His report makes clear the community menace of conditions allowed in the Negro quarters, and calls for the coöperation of the educated whites in upbuilding the homes, churches and schools of the Negroes. Reports like these, coming from a great and beloved university, are sure to leaven the thought of an entire state. Miss Stokes's gift, like that of Miss Jeanes, proves the wisdom of Northern philanthropists who choose Southerners in sympathy with Negro betterment to administer their gifts. Such gifts, so given, draw together the North and the South, as well as the two races in the South.

At the recent annual meeting of the Women's Missionary Council of the Southern Methodist Church the committee on Social Service brought in the following report, which was unanimously adopted :

" It shall be a duty of the Department of Social Service to promote the study of conditions and needs among the Negroes, locally, throughout the South ; also to arouse the women of our auxiliaries to a sense of their personal duty as Christian Southerners to meet the needs and ameliorate the conditions of those of this backward race who are in our midst by personal service and sympathy. We recommend the giving of this sympathy and service in any or all of the following ways :

"(1) By learning the needs of Negro Sunday-schools, teaching their Bible classes, training their teachers in modern Sunday-school methods, helping to grade their schools, and offering such other assistance as may be needed.

"(2) By assisting Negro women in forming and directing missionary societies in their churches, giving them information and other help, especially in regard to home mission work among the poorer classes of their own race.

"(3) By looking into the needs of Negro public schools, requiring of the public authorities that their premises be kept sanitary, helping to secure coloured teachers of a high grade, and favouring the introduction of industrial training.

"(4) By looking after the recreation, or lack of it, of Negro children and young people; by endeavouring to interest the Christian women of all denominations in securing for them opportunities for clean play in playgrounds supervised by good Negro women or men; and by securing coöperation with Negro Young Men's and Young Women's Associations where these exist.

"(5) By securing from boards of education permission to use Negro schoolhouses as community centres, organizing and assisting the better class of Negroes in each community to take charge of these community centres and supervise them for the pleasure and instruction of their own race. By interesting white people in the movement, securing white physicians and others to talk on personal and community hygiene, care of children, temperance, and other matters.

"(6) By visiting the local jails, by ascertaining the measure of justice accorded Negroes in the local courts, and by creating a sentiment for justice to youthful criminals whom wise treatment may reform.

"(7) By studying Negro housing conditions and their bearing on sickness, inefficiency, and crime; by bringing these conditions to the attention of the public; by insisting that the local authorities enforce in the Negro district the sanitary regulations of the community; by securing for Negroes a water supply sufficient for health and decency; by helping the Negroes of the better class to organize among their people civic clubs where the young may be trained in community cleanliness and righteousness.

"(8) By creating in the local white community higher ideals in regard to the relation between the two races; by standing for full and equal justice in all departments of life; by endeavouring to secure for the backward race not only the full measure of development of which they are capable, but the

unmolested possession and enjoyment of all
legitimate rewards of honest work; by standing, in short, for the full application to the
Negroes and to ourselves of the Mosaic law
of justice: 'Thou shalt love thy neighbour as
thyself.'"

There are four thousand auxiliaries in this
organization; and even though the work be
taken up slowly, it will spread.   The authorities at Paine College are urging upon the
church the establishment of a training school
for Negro missionaries and social workers
who may be employed by the whites as well
as by coloured churches in all these forms of
coöperative effort.   The need is so great we
can but trust it will be met.

The secretary for the Home Department
of the General Board of Missions of this
church is working along similar lines.   At
his instance the Alabama conference has
appointed a committee of ministers, laymen
and women, to look into the condition of
the Negroes within the bounds of the conference at all these points.   A consistent plan
of conference-wide help and coöperation is
expected to result; and such committees will
be asked for in the other conferences until all
have taken the matter up.

The deepest significance of all these movements in the various churches lies in the fact that they all look towards coöperation between the better classes of both races for the uplift of the Negro poor. It is impossible to serve the best interests of either race without this personal communication between the two. Where we have had a disposition to help the Negroes the attitude of the whites, both North and South, has been too often suggestive of that of the rich burgher in the play of Rip Van Winkle—"Give him a cold potato, and let him go." We have but given where he and we need that we should share.

There are notable individual exceptions, but many of even the well-educated Negroes are yet unequal to the task of achieving unaided the spiritual emancipation of their people. These need the forming and inspiring touch of educated whites.

In some of our Northern cities more or less money has been contributed for the uplift of the local Negro population through Y. M. C. A. work or otherwise ; but often, when the money is given, the Negroes are left quite to their own devices in trying to serve their people ; and the result is rarely all that it might be under a system of sympathetic coöperation between both races.

A Northern Y. M. C. A. worker, in speaking of this fact not long ago, said that the Negroes of the North did not desire coöperation, and frequently resented it when offered.

I think some Negroes in the South feel the same way, and are quick to repudiate the suggestion that the Negroes are not entirely competent to take full charge of Negro education and Negro uplift in general. They want white people to furnish the money, and leave them to direct the work.

That some Negroes are entirely equal to such a task cannot be truthfully denied. The logical deduction from this fact is that the race has capabilities of development far beyond the position some of us would permanently assign it. But it is idle to make claims which are not borne out by facts. The finest and strongest Negroes, I believe without a single exception, have come to their high development largely through contact with broad-minded, large-hearted white men and women. For years to come few of them are destined to reach that plane by any other process. I think on this point the real leaders in the South, white and black, are agreed.

There should be some white teachers in every state school for the higher education of Negroes ; but so far Alabama is the only state recognizing, in even a single institution, this statesmanlike and Christian principle. In Mississippi, however, whites have charge of the summer school for Negro teachers ; and in my home county of Richmond, in Georgia, the county superintendent supervises in person the yearly institute for Negro teachers, lecturing before them from time to time. This is probably not unusual.

The need for such service is threefold. As the more highly developed race we owe this help to the other race ; and unpaid spiritual debts issue, sooner or later, in spiritual bankruptcy. We must render such service for the sake of our own spiritual integrity. The Negroes need to receive all we can give them, that their own power to give, to their race and to the nation, may be enlarged. And beyond these needs is the fundamental necessity for both races to learn, however distinct they must remain racially, to work together in mutual respect, coöperating for the good of their common country, and for the kingdom of God on earth.

The exceptional Negro should be given the most responsible work as a teacher and leader of his people which his ability deserves. But the race would be superhuman if in fifty years of freedom it had become capable of taking its future entirely into its own hands. Some Negroes do not recognize this fact, and are quick to resent white assistance as white interference ; and especially to distrust any measure or method which emphasizes the need for discipline of mind or spirit. Surely we are responsible here. Our long indifference weighs heavily against us ; and our assistance, where offered, is too often tinctured—or impregnated—with condescension. If Christ had come to us that way I think we would be savages still. However fine it may look on the outside, there is no lifting force in any condescending deed. When we set about our task in that entire simplicity and self-unconsciousness which are a necessary part of the spirit of Christian service, we will be oftener surprised by the depth of the response evoked than by a disposition to reject our help. Money alone, though we poured it into institutions for the Negroes like water, cannot settle our debt. The world around, the debt of the privileged involves their personality.

One of the straws which show our new consciousness of this fact blew across my path not long ago as I was returning from a trip to the North. In a travellers' chat with another passenger the subject of women's club-work came up ; and my companion, knowing nothing of my own interests, told me of her recent experience as president of the federated clubs of her home town, a thriving city in North Carolina. The club-women had decided on a Clean-up Day, when it occurred to her that in order to make it a real cleaning day the city should be cleaned, and not merely that fraction of it which least needed cleansing. So she pro-posed to the club-women that for the health of their own households, as well as for other obvious reasons, they should invite the lead-ers of all the Negro women's societies to a conference, get them interested in the move-ment, and have a Clean-up Day which would leave the city clean. They expected perhaps a dozen Negro women, and seventy came. The mayor of the city and the president of the Board of Health addressed the gather-ing, and then the women talked, white and black.

"And you'd have been as astonished as we were if you'd heard those Negroes," she declared. "Some of them knew as much about parliamentary proceedings as we did ; and they were so sensible, they talked so well, they were so glad to do all they could ! —And I tell you," she added with a little laugh, " when it came to cleaning up, we had to hustle to keep up with them.—We don't expect much sickness in town this summer : the place—the whole place—is clean."

And Negroes do not respond to ideals? Let those who give them a chance—a growing group among us—testify.

This North Carolina club is not alone. On the Women's Club page of the *Atlanta Constitution* I read recently, in a single issue, accounts of three Georgia clubs which are cooperating with the Negroes of their respective cities to keep their towns clean and healthful.

The annual meetings of the Virginia State Board of Charities and Correction are open to both races. The Negroes report there their work among their own people ; and the attitude of the Board is one of solicitude and helpfulness towards all dependents and delinquents in the commonwealth, rather than towards those of one race.

It is a Virginia town, too, which is demonstrating the wisdom of another form of cooperation ; a form so simple, so needed, so obviously Christian, that one feels it should only be known to be adopted. I learned of it from a chance acquaintance whose relatives live in the town. The Protestant ministers of

STILLMAN INSTITUTE, TUSCALOOSA, ALA.

the town, he said, both white and black, are members of the Ministers' Alliance. They meet once a month, as brothers of Him who came to serve all races and all classes of men, to pray and talk and plan for the spiritual uplift of the whole community. If Christ came again in the flesh, surely nowhere could He feel more at home than in a meeting-place like that.

It is puzzling that the local churches, of all denominations, all over the South, should fail as they do in leadership in this matter. Every large denomination has officially gone on record, in its highest legislative body, as recognizing the common brotherhood of the races, the common duty of the strong race to serve the weak one. No voice has been publicly lifted, in any denomination, to controvert this doctrine. White ministers have, undoubtedly, the kindliest feelings to Negroes. None of them, I think, would hesitate to accept gladly any invitation to speak or preach to a black audience. In my own denomination, when one speaks to a conference body of ministers about our duty to the Negroes there is, of recent years, a deep, and often moving, response ; and the presiding bishop never fails to press the duty home. And we are not double-faced, nor cowards. But I doubt if, in any state, a dozen ministers could be found, in all denominations put together, who make a practice of preaching, even once in two or three years, about race relations, or our duty to our black poor, or the connection between the Negro quarters of our cities and the interests of the kingdom of God. Yet these things enter into the warp and woof of daily life in the South, and help or hinder the growth in Christian character of every member of every church.

It is true the leaders of the South's best thought and action regarding the Negroes are church-members, grown up under Southern preachers; and in at least three great denominations the head of the work for Negroes is a minister, officially backed by his church. Yet the pulpits of the South rarely speak of those problems which press upon us all, and for which there is no solution outside the teachings of Christ. In this as in other things, the country over, the churches have yielded their crown of leadership to members who must do much of their work along lines largely ignored by the rank and file of the ministry.

Yet there are exceptions, each one a shining example of the leadership possible to our pulpits. Not long ago, after an outburst of race antagonism which was being chronicled and condemned in all the papers, I asked a Negro from a neighbouring state if such feeling existed in his section.

"No, ma'am, it don't," he answered emphatically ; "not for a long time."

"Then it used to exist ? "

"Oh, yes'm. We ain't had a thing but trouble till these last few years."

"What stopped it ? "

"A white preacher stopped it. He thought some of the things done weren't right ; and he got all the white preachers in town to agree to preach about Christ's way of treating coloured folks, all on the same day. They all did it again a month later, and once or twice more that year. And as long as he stayed there they all preached about it together that way, a time or two each year ; and there ain't any trouble since. I heard tell two or three white folks got mad about it ; but the preachers stuck it out. And now all the white folks treat us right, and we all are behaving better, and everybody is prospering a heap better than they used to."

Instances like this will multiply as our social conscience quickens. A fresh, clean wind stirs over the South before which old mists of prejudice are lifting. Insufficient

and halting as the work of the churches has
been, it has yet testified to the Christian
duty of service and the Christian doctrine of
brotherhood.   That all the churches must at
some points, perhaps at many, be readjusted
to conditions few who love them will deny: but
in England, and in America, North and South,
it is the churches which have created that
social conscience which some deem all-suffi-
cient without the churches, and at which the
churches themselves sometimes look askance,
as at a rival which would usurp their domin-
ion.   The Southern Sociological Congress is
the first South-wide expression of this nascent
conscience; and no one who attended the
Congress meetings, in Nashville or in Atlanta,
could fail to be impressed with the religious
spirit in which men of many faiths had met
to consider their common duties to the unprivileged of the South.

Out of the first meeting of the section on
Race Relations came the appointment of
a Southern University Commission on the
Negro, with a representative from nearly
every Southern state university.   This commission met for organization in December,
1912.   It reported to the Atlanta Congress a
broad outline of investigation to be undertaken in regard to conditions—religious,

educational, hygienic, economic and civic;
the duty of whites in improving these conditions; and the ideal of race-relations towards
which the South should work. No one who
has heard these men speak, as several have
already done in public, can doubt that large
hearts and clear brains are at work upon the
whole subject in a spirit of justice and service.

This is not the place to discuss the Congress at large; but it furnished many evidences of a social conscience at last astir on
all community interests. The sectional meetings on Race Relations were a dream come
true—a dream of a new South, with the old
spirit of sympathy once more in the heart of
the strong, and hands of human brotherhood
held out to the weaker race. The privileged
South has at last opened its doors of counsel
and invited the unprivileged to enter in and
talk over, men with men, the needs and duties
which confront them both in making the land
a home of justice and opportunity for all.

But that was not the whole story. With
Southern white and Southern black speaking
from the same platform, and seeing in so
many things eye to eye at last, were men of
that other class so long misunderstood and
misjudged among us—the men of the North
who came long ago to meet a great human

need among those whom we, for the dark time being, had closed our hearts against. North and South and black and white met there, and pledged their common service to a common humanity, a common country, and a common God.

We stood, for those brief days, on one of those mountain tops from which the end is seen, near and beautiful and real. Afterwards, one turns to the rugged path again, and faces the long, long road. But the end is still real and beautiful, and as certain as Love itself. And as for nearness, shall one measure the life of the Race of Man by one's own narrow years; or the world-wide victory that awaits by one's tiny measure of personal failure or success? Though we ourselves pass not over, yet shall our brothers possess the land, and dwell there.

Sometimes a biologist, studying tissues under the microscope, will stain some cells and not others, that he may the better unravel some of life's obscure interactions.

I think God has done that in the South, dyeing our weak ones black, that it may be clear to the most careless what the weak have to suffer from the selfishness of the strong. Once we begin to see, it ought to be easier for us than for others to learn community righteousness, because the effects of evil are made so plain among us. And those who look on from afar should, rather than criticize us, watch more closely their own community life, where the strong may wrong the weak in less spectacular fashion.

It may be long before it is all stopped. The evil is great everywhere ; and we of the South have been slow to start our part of the fight against it. But we have started now, at last—not as individuals only, as heretofore ; but as a constantly-growing group of Southern folk who feel the common obligation of those who have to serve those who have not.

And having taken these first steps in recognition of our share of a world-task the main peculiarity of our Southern situation has vanished. For we have joined hands, we too, at last, with the privileged of earth elsewhere, to set free those without privilege ; to serve our neighbour, not according to the colour of his skin, but according to his need.

# VII

## THOSE WHO COME AFTER US

**B**EING parents is the deepest thing in life. It runs away back of humanity, out into the wild, free places, where the bird broods high in air, and the weed pours all its being into its seed, and dies. It is doubtless this blood-kinship stirring in us when we yearn for the woods, and the mountains, and the sea ; some inarticulate inner consciousness knows all these as homes of life, our common heritage, our common trust. With all the weight of suffering of those to whom the highest honours of that trust have been committed, and who have, as yet, failed to be worthy of them, we turn back to these haunts of simpler and more loyal forms of life for rest, and for strength and courage for the long road our feet have yet to go.

Parenthood is a thing to bind all life in one. It is not merely that nothing human is foreign to us afterwards : no life that grows by sacrifice is alien ; and that is all the life there is.

It seems the miracle of the ages that we,

on the summit of life, we humans, should have made this thing unclean : that the power to pass on the torch of life, to call out of nothingness those who shall shape the future of the race—that this, of all things, should be the force to make men beasts again, and to build for multitudes of the women of all races an age-long hell on earth.

At least one good should come of it : it should bind the women of the world in one, Being a woman goes deeper than being of this race or that, or of this or that social station.  Red, yellow, or black, or white, we carry the world's sins on our shoulders, its degradation and anguish in our hearts.  It all falls on the women, the lust, the degradation, the suffering.  And what is a keener agony, a more intolerable shame, it falls on the women's daughters, whom they won in the valley of death.  Have we not reason to stand together, we women of the world ?  A Chinese girl hawked publicly by her owner on the streets of Shanghai, an Indian maid betrayed in the forest, girls of our own race by scores of thousands, Negro girls whom men of no race reverence—where is the difference ?  They are women, women all ; and women bore them : women should stand together for the womanhood of the world.

It burns like fire when first we grasp that truth. It is inevitable, in the beginning, when the knowledge of broken lives first flares in our faces, and we reach hands of fellowship to draw some poor outcast back into the circle of human sympathy again, that women's standing together should mean to us their standing against the men. We are quick to hate, when we are young ; and men are an easy mark. Nothing excuses them to us, nothing palliates. An honoured father, a brother whom we trust, a husband well-be-loved—these are the accidents of the sex ; creatures in whom, by some great miracle, a touch of their mothers' souls has turned dross to gold : but for men ——. The sharpest trial of faith is no mental question to a woman ; it comes straight from the heart of life, terrible and fierce : Would a good God make women as women are made, and shut them up in the same world with men ?

And then, into such a woman's life, is sent a little son. He shall defy the law of his sex ; he shall be pure, though all men else follow the common path.

She lives her son's life, and so she wins the freedom of his world. It takes imagination, and patience, and sympathy, and time. But when he begins to run with other boys she has his confidence; and so she learns, as we all must, by love, and not by hate.

What chance have they, these little boys, any more than the girls whose lives they poison? Before they know the meaning of words or acts their lives are poisoned, too. We care for everything about them, bodies and minds, except this highest thing, which we call unclean, and hide. It is not a question of a child's being taught or not taught; he learns, as surely as he lives and breathes. It is a question of how he shall be taught: in truth and cleanness, or in lies and filth. And because this power is the highest intrusted to us, because its perversion causes more misery and degradation than everything else put together, the right training of children in matters of sex is a basal necessity for the world's progress in righteousness. Shall we dare to remain prudes when we see what silence costs our children, sons and daughters both? Love takes no account of such childish shrinking, however much love may feel it: love serves the beloved unashamed, and at any cost. And love can find a way.

The future of both races in the South is more deeply concerned in this than in any other one thing. For to the pure all achievement is possible; and for the impure rottenness and decay are certain. There is no reason whatever for believing that any one country or section sins above the rest in this matter. Where two races of different colours dwell side by side, one strong, one weak, the evidences of sin are not to be hidden : yet the sin exists no less, though less visibly, where strong and weak are of one skin. But there is no section of any country which is not implicated in the authorized statement of physicians of world-repute that seventy per cent. of the men of Christendom are, or have been, sufferers from vice-diseases. The meaning of such a statement staggers the mind : the stunted bodies and souls of children, women's long-drawn-out torments, the maiming of mind and flesh, the perverts, the paupers, the insane ! Shall we be ashamed to remove burdens like these from those who shall follow us ? Shall we shrink from sending the children of the South out unhandicapped, strong of body and pure in mind, to build the homes of the future ; homes where white folk dwell, where black folk dwell, each secure from wrong and from fear ?

For it can be so. There is a new day breaking. Old evils, hoary with the centuries until we have accepted them as inseparable from life itself, are being challenged, defied.

The German Government believes the purity of young men not impossible of attainment. It orders the instruction in sex hygiene of every college student in the land. At a recent annual meeting of the American Medical Association one of their leading speakers, in a formal address, called on the churches of America to aid the doctors in their fight against the social evil by the teaching of sex hygiene. The doctors stood long, many of them, for the necessity of " wild oats." As an association they have now endorsed the movement for social purity as a necessity for personal and social health. That great, conservative organization, the Church of England, has undertaken a year's-long campaign against the social evil, with the avowed intention of uprooting it from English life.

Time was when we thought yellow fever was providential. A providence which made yellow fever an integral part of the scheme of things would be benevolent indeed beside a providence which made this loathsome cancer a necessity of human life. We had yellow fever because we had not learned to destroy the breeding-places of the pests which carry it. We have the social evil for exactly the same reason.

Its breeding-places are in the unclean

thoughts of children and young people who were made to think cleanly. There is nothing more wonderful, more sacrificially pure, than the great law of life by which life comes from life, and like from like, strong life from pure, and weak from foul, which runs through all the organisms of earth. When a child begins to question he needs—and she—not lies, but the clean truth. If the mother does not answer somebody else will; and then the poison will be at work.

A child can be taught *unconsciously* to reverence the life-giving power which he holds in trust. When the stress of temptation comes, swift and sharp, he may find himself prepared. He need not battle in the dark, ignorant of himself, of the meaning of life, of its dangers and rewards. A girl can be protected in all purity, that in time of danger she may so remain. Our parents did not know : but for an intelligent parent to send children out to-day defenseless against the contagions of school life is a neglect the child may find it impossible to forgive.

There is a little book by Ellen Torrelle, published by Heath, called "Plant and Animal Children, and How They Grow." One need not be botanist or biologist to make its stories clear to children's minds; and a child who understands its facts is unconsciously fortified against uncleanness. There is no room for impurity concerning the origin of life, not because it has been inveighed against, but because its possible place has been filled with thoughts beautiful and pure. Another book, which all adults and every adolescent boy should read, is Lavinia Dock's " Hygiene and Morality," published by the Putnams. In addition to these, and for many purposes, parents would do well to read Stanley Hall's " Youth," published by Appleton. There are many other books, large and small, a list of which may be had from the National Vigilance Committee, in New York.

The time is not far distant when the teaching of such books as Miss Torrelle's will be obligatory in the earlier grades of the public schools ; and when that is secured for those who shall come after us, the poor man's home, North, South and West, will be safer— yes, and the homes of the privileged too. For this hideous infection can never be confined, while it exists at all, to one economic class, or to this or that locality. It breeds misery and degradation for the community, just so far as it breeds at all.

But education is not the only measure ; nor need we wait for a new generation to grow

up to introduce wide-spread reform. Health
laws should compel all physicians, as they already do those of a few states in other sections, to report not only cases of the lesser
contagions, such as scarlet fever, diphtheria
and the like ; but also the far more dangerous contagions of the vice-diseases. With
this law goes a second, requiring a physician's certificate to the applicant's freedom
from contagious disease before a marriage
license can be issued. These laws are being
widely advocated by physicians of the highest standing, by social workers everywhere,
and by many health officers, parents, educators and ministers.

Another law urgently needed in many
states, and in no section more than in our
own, is one raising the age of consent to at
least eighteen years. In some of our Southern states it is ten years. The mere statement
of such a fact would come as a shock to
any but the most nascent social conscience.
What of morality can we hope to evolve in
the classes most in need of morality, white and
black, when the defenseless childhood of the
poor is held so cheap *by law ?*

But beyond all this, what can the privileged
mothers do for those unprivileged, the strong
to help the weak ? For women should stand

together, for the manhood and the womanhood of the world. Mothers cannot, if they would, break the tie which binds them to both sexes, to the whole human race.

Privilege exists for one end only—that it may become the common servitor of all. We pray such curious prayers sometimes, in the pulpit and out of it—prayers which automatically prevent their own fulfillment. We are so anxious for "especial" care and good, for "peculiar" blessings, for things which would mark us as a folk apart, or a family, or even an individual, sheltered from ordinary trials, lifted above the multitude who hunger, separated from the common lot, favoured of heaven beyond other folk!

A god who would answer prayers like those it should be beneath one's self-respect to pray to. If he be not equally the God of all flesh, he is no god for any flesh to petition. For there is a deep sense in which God Himself must be thought of in terms of humanity, so that no one who seeks fullness of life, which is fullness of love, may dare ask any protection, any mercy, any good for any aspect of our many-sided life, the giving of which would imply anything whatever "especial" in the sense that it is not open, to the limit of his need, to the least of all flesh who may ask for it.

But more than that. When we get this background of prayer in our minds, this true perspective of our own needs in relation to those of the rest of the world, we see the basis of justice on which the fulfilling of those needs must rest. It is for lack of justice in our petitions that we have so largely been, in all the ages,

> " Bafflers of our own prayers, from youth to life's
>     last scenes."

Mothers should understand, because love costs them more, and so they should be wiser in its ways. There can be no safe basis for prayer for one's child except this basis of justice. If we desire protection for our daughters, or purity for our sons, strong bodies for them and trained minds, a place for happy play, freedom and joy in work, a life made rich by love and service, it is strange that we should dare to ask these things of a just God except as we pledge our full strength to effort to secure like good for all the children, the world around, to whom it is denied.

What things that we desire for our children do Negro children lack? I do not mean the luxuries, nor even many of the comforts of life : but those basal necessities to any clean, efficient, hopeful life, however humble and poor: abundant water and fresh air, with a knowledge of their uses ; houses where homes are possible ; sanitary surroundings ; school training which really trains ; a chance for clean play ; mothers who can approximate a mother's duties; religious instruction related to daily life. Without these things, what kind of people are they foredoomed to be? And whose is the responsibility?

But more than that. Women make the standards for every community in our land. North, South and West, community morals and ideals are exactly what, consciously or unconsciously, the consciences of the privileged women of that community permit. If the morality of the daughters of the very poor is to be safeguarded anywhere, it must be done by the privileged women primarily. And our very poor are black.

We need, in the first place, to see the women of our poor as women first, and black afterwards. We need a new respect for them in our own minds, as children of the one Father, even as we. We need more faith in the possibilities of the poorest life which is born with a capacity, however limited, for divine things. We need to use our imaginations, to put ourselves in the Negro woman's place.   We will find the exercise as broadening to our own lives as it will be beneficial to the Negro's.   We need to think of Negro womanhood as sacred, as the womanhood of all the world must be.   Thinking so, we will begin to honour its possibilities, and try to bring them out.   And if we hold up that standard, our men will come to it ; they cannot help themselves.   It is women who rule the world—or who can rule it, always, if only they will stand together.   It is not merely that we have the men when they are babies. Beyond that tremendous fact men are dependent on women as women are not upon men. When women fix the terms on which men may secure their companionship and their love men must meet the conditions : they have no escape.   Only, women must stand together, for womanhood, and for the race.

Let us plan the future of the South we love under a wide sky.   Let us plan, not for our children merely, nor for our race, else can the plans never bear full fruit.   All that we want for our own let us plan for the children of the South, rich and poor, high and low, black and white : strong bodies, clean minds, hands skilled to labour, hearts just and kind and wise.   Children do not grow like that of themselves, any more than roses grow double in the swamps : it is the children's power to respond to cultivation which lays upon us the duty of giving it.

I knew a family once where there were several normal children, and one little child, the youngest, whom epilepsy had reduced almost to idiocy. He was most repulsive to me when I first saw him, before I understood. He seemed that awful thing which some imagine they see in the world's undeveloped races—something in human shape without human capacity.

But his parents loved him so much ! Their tenderness never failed for him, their care never abated. They loved the other children dearly, too ; but this child needed them so much : they loved him according to his need.

Think of them for a moment—the hordes of the unprivileged of every race ; those cut off from joy ; the folk whose years are filled only with a great emptiness, with immeasurable ignorance and want ; the mass of men and women, really, the vast majority of the human race. And God so loves the world—just so : according to the need.

# VIII

## THE GREAT ADVENTURE

I CANNOT close this little book without a word concerning those whose childhood is behind them, and who are soon to take their places in that great array of toilers whose hands are moulding the world's life in the present. Life looms before them as the Great Adventure, wherein difficulties and trials may await them, but which, in some unknown, far-off place, shall issue in achievement; in something which shall win them a place and honour which their own effort has secured for them, well-deserved.

We older people, the mass of us at least, look on as the raw recruits pass out, and smile, some of us kindly, some pityingly, some with bitterness, seeing their young enthusiasms, the high resolves and hopes which drive them, the gleam of the half-formed ideals which lure them on. Life will grip these over-confident children, we think, and trim them all to one sober pattern by the time they reach middle age. They will learn fast enough to accept its drudgery and to bow to its yoke. In the valley of old age they will stand much as their fathers stood, moulded by life, not moulding it, their laughter done ; strong perhaps, but strong chiefly to accept and to bear the inevitable.

Is that the normal end of youth, the natural outcome of the Great Adventure ; or are we so ill-adjusted to our environment that the abnormal is the usual and the normal the uncommon outcome of the quest ?

Surely power is never intended for futility, and only ignorance can unmoved see it turned to waste. Yet if we measure in terms of human energy the advance of any one generation, and compare it with the force originally applied to secure advance, with that fund of energy, of hope and joy which we sum up as youth, the waste of power is staggering. It is only the smallest fraction of it which has been utilized : the rest has been absorbed by frictions which have largely wrecked the generators themselves. The energy of youth has gone to the destruction of all that makes youth young and wonderful. The one-time possessors of it stand broken, exhausted, numbed, in the valley of the Shadow ; and the world they intended to lift has turned by a hair's breadth, and no more.

Yet some find youth but a gateway into a life which knows no age. Their bodies grow older, but only to reveal to the puzzled looker-on how very little years are concerned with either age or youth. Down to the very last their hearts are young, their fine enthusiasms unspent, their sympathies quick and keen, their joy unbroken, their hope a light no shadow can quench. Out of a long life filled, as we may know, chiefly with drudgeries and trials like our own, they come with young, eager eyes, out of which still looks the spirit of high adventure. Their message to youth is one of courage and hope :

> " Grow old along with me !
> The best is yet to be,
> The last of life, for which the first was made."

Surely that is the normal attitude of age, the natural outcome of youth and endeavour and hope. Wherever we see it, even the dullest of us, it appeals to some deep thing in us which, despite all our pessimism, justifies it, even against our will. It is so beautiful we know it must be true : all age was meant to be like that.

But how shall youth attain it ? What subtle force has turned one life into this flashing diamond, and left another only dull, black

coal, though they are both alike compact of
a common humanity, and share its common
lot ?   How shall we gear the spirit of youth,
how band the individual to life in such manner that he may serve it without being broken
by it ; that he may drive on towards the fulfillment of his dreams, nor lose his hope, nor
despair of the far achievement, but keep even
in age

"The rapture of the forward view,"

and the spirit of immortal joy ?   If life be the
Great Adventure how may one achieve it
greatly, and know one's self a victor, even in
the midnight of defeat ?

One must live the normal human life to
secure all that.   We cannot expect human
issues from a life lived on the animal's plane.
An animal which is only an animal may come
to the best of itself in isolation, an unrelated
unit of its race.   A young colt, or pig, or
calf, left on an island where no other animal
life existed, but provided with food and shelter
the primal animal needs, would be as perfect
an animal as one reared in association with
droves of its own kind.   But a creature which
is an animal and something more never
comes to the best of itself when only those
needs are met which may be satisfied in

isolation. There are several authentic records of wolf-raised human young, and they have all reverted to the animal type. Kipling's Mowgli, fascinating as he is, is inspired by his creator's own imagination ; a real Mowgli could never have taken his place among human beings again, even on the edge of the jungle. Real wolf-children are like the Wild Man of Auvergne, whom a wise-hearted scientist laboured with so patiently over a hundred years ago. Cut off from human association the human in us atrophies beyond recall. For the primal law of human life is that to be truly human it must be shared with its kind.

When we get down to principles of life we are prone, unconsciously, to fall into Biblical phraseology ; the roots of principles seem to run in that direction. It is literally true that no man liveth or dieth to himself : humanity is made that way. Whatever lives and dies some other way is not human, but animal. We live, we draw on the sources of life, we nourish and strengthen it, in exact measure as we share it with the race.

This is the secret of our wasted joy, our lost enthusiasms, our broken hopes : we have failed of the normal human life, the life of race-association, the life of brotherhood,

POOR HOUSING CONDITIONS IN THE SOUTH

234B

The drop of water has lost itself and perished in the desert of individual desire, instead of finding itself in the stream of community life which trickles down through ever-widening associations to the great ocean of the Life of Man.  In a most vital sense, the normal man, full-grown, has nothing to do with sections or boundaries, except as they help him to understand those of his brothers whom they dwarf and bind.  For himself, he is a citizen of the world ; and nothing in human life is foreign to him, past, present, or to come. The sense of race-life in himself, one atom of the mass, of the race-life whose laws govern atom and mass alike, opens all life to him, steadies his courage, heals his wounds, renews his youth, and feeds the flame of hope.

One's individual joy may be clouded so easily, and so soon ; it is such a small, weak thing, taken by itself.  It is part of the law of life that it should be so ; for he who would be man and not animal must be welded into one with his fellows; and love itself is not enough, without pain.

Suffering is so inexplicable, at first ; it sets one apart while life sweeps by.  But one has to be apart to get the perspective of life, to see small and great in their true proportions, to learn the unshakable things, and to get one's own small personality properly related to them. At first, with all of us, it is the old cry : Was ever sorrow like unto my sorrow, or difficulty like to mine?—That is the cry of ignorance, of weakness, of selfishness, of egotism and provincialism, the world around. It has gone up in all ages, and will go up for ages yet to come.

But if one turns from one's atom-sorrow for a moment to take the race-wide, age-long look, one sees that always, everywhere, such sorrows have been. They are part of the race-lot. And everywhere there are, and have been, men and women who have borne them bravely, and lived and died without bitterness or complaint. Their lives are part of the race inheritance ; their courage lifts us up. What man has done we can do ; they fought their battles not for themselves alone. The strength of the race flows into us : we too can greatly bear ; we too can wear the badge of courage to hearten those who stumble by the way. If the race must advance through suffering we will walk that path. We would not be exempt, cut off. Shall we alone, of all the multitudes, bear no scars ?

Personal success means something different after that. The Adventure itself is different ; greater, and more worth while. The quest one would achieve is fullness of life; the path to it matters not so much. And fullness of life is never personal, but human. One has cast in one's lot with the race; and in doing that, whatever struggles are yet to come, the visible can no longer master the unseen. One is delivered from that poverty of soul.

The greatest danger of education is that it may be twisted, just like ignorance, to the service of intellectual arrogance, and so may breed spiritual decay. We all need world-association; but especially those need it who are unusually gifted, that they may escape the catastrophe of an emasculating egotism. The man who is the mental superior of all his associates can neutralize that dangerous misfortune only by finding his equals and his superiors wherever, in the race-life, they have blossomed to the light. He must break the shackles of time and place to commune with the mind of the race; and through that communion must learn the humility inevitable to him who measures himself by universal, rather than by provincial standards. Thus disciplined, he may add his atom of force to the race-impetus towards righteousness without pride and without shame.

In such an association the race gains in-

finitesimally : the individual gains the emancipation of his individuality, and walks henceforth at liberty and with joy.  The sting is
gone from the thwarting narrowness of
life ; for the small task, set in its large relations, is at once worth while.  He is lifted
enough above pettiness, his own and that of
others, to know it for what it is, and to be
safe from the hurt of it.  Personal defeat, too,
loses its bitterness.  However his individual
life goes down in ruins, the great powers of
truth and brotherhood to which he has committed himself remain ; that for which he
struggled will triumph yet.  His life, defeated
though it be, is part of the victory of the race.

One's sense of joy is widened.  Indeed, it
has to be, or one could not endure the shar-
ing of the sorrows of mankind.  But the race
is achieving, always.  Each day sees something done which stirs the blood in the long

" World-war of dying flesh against the life."

Each day somewhere the curtains of the
dark are lifted, and new knowledge gives
new light.  Each day men and women of all
races, plain, simple folk like ourselves, are
meeting difficulties with high hearts, unknown
heroes in unguessed fights.  And we are a
part of all of it ; we all work to one end.

Seen from the narrow window of a detached personal experience, life is confusing, baffling, coming no-whence, going no-whither, bound blind to the wheel of chance, and broken as it turns. It is the race-look which reveals the truth. The confusions are temporary, local, born of continued readjustments to higher levels. Whatever its weakness or its ignorance, life tends up. Men die, and races pass ; but Man rises. One is no longer afraid of changes, though to the atom's unrelated consciousness the very foundations seem threatened. There is a Power that guides : and in the end, that which was planned from the beginning shall be.

So it is that the consciousness of race-life forms the rich background of our own small existence, giving depth and colour to our thin personalities, enriching and beautifying the poorest life which may be set against it. It saves us, too, in those times which come to all of us, when a sense of the futility of life descends upon us like a great black frost, shrivelling effort which had promised fruitage, and numbing the sources of energy and hope. It is then that we warm our hearts at the hearthstone of humanity, folded deep in the consciousness of a life which bears our tiny being on its breast, and which moves unerringly, if slowly, through seed-time and harvest, summer and winter, to one sure, high, far-off goal.

But the race-life is not only shelter and solace in days of suffering or defeat: it is also our inspiration and joy.

To him who walks in love among his neighbours in the little happenings of every day, and out into love's wider paths of community service, there comes, sooner or later, a day when every cloud is withdrawn; when he sees back to the low beginnings of life, and on, to its far fulfillment. He sees humanity in its first home, there in the mud and slime of things, pushing feebly forward here and there, driven by sharp necessity, inch by inch, dyeing the path with its own blood, yet slowly accumulating, out of its own sufferings, forces which purify and lift it. It begins to live not by bread alone: each least advance is purchased for it by some sacrificial life. From every rank of the vast savage mass the Givers come, offering up man's life for the Life of Man. Seer and sage and warrior, king and peasant, master and slave, mothers whom no man may number, they pour out life like water, and thereby fructify the barren souls of the multitude, and create ideals for the race.

What else should life be for? What trace is left of all the beast-lives lived solitary in the mass, smothered in egotism, cut off by self-ishness—what, but an added weight for these, the Givers, to lift?

Love is the motive force of life, and it gathers, more and more. Out of the mass emerge those races whose growing powers endue them with the greatest capacity for sacrifice, for following the ideal at all costs. However the majority of even these foremost races may fall short, however the hard-won earnings of the race are perverted by the many to personal ends, Love does make headway, slowly. All that the Givers would win for men of liberty, of knowledge, of justice, of joy, filters down unceasingly from class to class, until already some of the most precious things of life grow as common to them all as the air we breathe.

Is not the life of the Givers well-spent? In all the long, long ages is anything else so well worth while? They lost life only to find it; and being dead, they yet speak to us. Their voices go up

"A cry above the conquered years,"

and the deepest things in us stir in answer. In such an hour we know life for what it really is—the power which comes in all its glorious fullness only to those who hold it in trust for every soul that needs.

Is there room for egotism any more, or pride—those two chief stranglers of human joy ? Can one be afraid of "losing caste" by service ? One lives in a world so far removed from all that—the world of fullness of life ; a world wide with freedom, and rich with love, and bright with victory, however one's own small fortunes may rise or fall. For the soul has come into its own, and found its home, close to the heart of God, in the needs of humankind.

Shall we fail of this wide, free life here in the South because of old prejudice, and black skins over the needs? Shall we, who were once so low, who have risen, not through decades but through centuries, risen by life poured out, reaping our gain from the sacrifice of the ages, heirs in direct spiritual succession of all foregone races of men, shall we, of all mankind, withhold our bread from the hungry, and justice from the oppressed?

We are so ready to use what we have inherited, not for service, but for pride. If humanity be like the earth, we say, we are its mountain-peaks, the Himalayas of the race.—But the seas rolled over the mountains

once ; and seas may roll there again.    To
the long look, the true look, the look to which
a thousand years are but a day, mountains
have risen before, and have disappeared.

> " The hills are shadows, and they flow
>      From form to form, and nothing stands ;
>      They melt like mists, the solid lands,
> Like clouds they shape themselves, and go."

The earth alone abides, mother of all mountains that ever were, or will be.

If life is not to grow dull to us, young or
old, or its glamour fade; if we are one day
to stand on those heights which belong to
age rather than on the dull, flat barrens at
their base ; if life is to remain the Great
Adventure, full of promise and wonder even
in that last twilight before the eternal dawn,
we must live it normally, through the years,
despising no service that sets another heart
at ease or opens a rift of opportunity to the
poorest and least.

The beginnings of all great things are
small.    Indeed, most great things are small
all the way through, made up of trifles, and
great only in their accumulated results.    Only
the fewest people have great gifts or opportunities ; and often they are not the ones who
achieve the greatest things.    A world filled

with ordinary folk and based on justice necessitates a broad path straight from the commonplaces of every day up to the highest heights. And we have just that. The basal necessity is not knowledge, nor power, but love ; and that is the greatest and the most freely attained of all human possessions. Rich or poor or ignorant or learned, the Great Adventure shall be achieved by all who walk in love.

*Printed in the United States of America*

# SOCIOLOGY AND PRACTICAL RELIGION

*CLARA E. LAUGHLIN*　　　　*Author of*
*"Everybody's Lonesome"*

## The Work-A-Day Girl

A Study of Present Day Conditions. Illustrated, 12mo, cloth, net $1.50.

Few writers to-day have given more serious and sympathetic consideration to the difficulties which beset the American working girl. The book is frank and outspoken, but not too much so for there is need of plain talk on a matter so vital to our social welfare.

*FREDERIC J. HASKIN*　　　　*Author of*
*"The American Government"*

## The Immigrant : An Asset and a Liability

12mo, cloth, net $1.25.

"Persons are asking how they may best do their duty and their whole duty to those coming to our shores. This book is a valuable light on the subject. It is full of facts and it is a capable and conscientious study as to the meaning of the facts. Any thoughtful person will find here much valuable material for study and the book is calculated to do much good."—*Herald and Presbyter.*

*CHARLES STELZLE*

## The Gospel of Labor

12mo, cloth, net 50c.

"Sometimes it is a short sermonette, sometimes it is a story, but every one of the thirty-three chapters is a presentation in terse, graphic English of some phase of the gospel of labor by a man who knows the life of labor from the inside. A stimulating message for the laboring man, and many valuable suggestions for those who desire to enter into his life in the most helpful way."—*Presbyterian Advance.*

*PROFESSOR JAMES R. HOWERTON*

## The Church and Social Reform

12mo, cloth, net 75c.

"In a succinct and yet very thorough manner the author discusses the fundamentals of this present-day problem of the relation of the church to social reform, and the obligations entailed. The volume is an exceptionally helpful one, serving to clear the atmosphere and show the way out."—*Christian World.*

*P. MARION SIMMS*

## What Must the Church Do to Be Saved ?

The Necessity and Possibility of the Unity of Protestantism. 12mo, cloth, net $1.50.

From a first-hand observation the author brings together a body of facts which emphasize strongly the necessity for a practical union among the denominations of the Church of Christ in America to fulfill her mission. The remedies proposed by the author are set forth with a reasonableness and straightforwardness which invite the respect of all readers.

# FICTION WITH A PURPOSE

*RUPERT HUGHES*

## Miss 318 and Mr. 37

Illustrated, 12mo, cloth, net 75c.

Miss 318 has met her affinity. In this latest story of how she captured him in the person of a New York fire laddie, "Number 37," Mr. Hughes has surpassed himself. The narrative is full of the same characters, humor, department store lingo and vital human interest of MISS 318.

*MARY ELIZABETH SMITH*

## In Bethany House

A Story of Social Service. 12mo, cloth, net $1.25.

"Without any plot at all the book would still be worth reading; with its earnestness, its seriousness of purpose, its health optimism, its breadth of outlook, and its sympathetic insight into the depths of the human heart."—*N. Y. Times*

*MARGARET E. SANGSTER*

## Eastover Parish    Cloth, net $1.00.

A new story by Margaret Sangster is an "event" among a wide circle of readers. Mary E. Wilkins places Mrs. Sangster as "a legitimate successor to Louise M. Alcott as a writer of meritorius books for girls, combining absorbing story and high moral tone." Her new book is a story of "real life and real people, of incidents that have actually happened in Mrs. Sangster's life."

*THOMAS D. WHITTLES*

## The Parish of the Pines

The Story of Frank Higgins, the Lumber-Jack's Sky Pilot. Illustrated, 12mo, cloth, net $1.00.

Norman Duncan, author of "The Measure of a Man," calls this "Walking boss of the Sky-route Company," "a man's Christian doing an admirable work in the Woods of the Northwest." The narrative has the ozone, and the spicyness of the great pine forests in which the scenes are laid.

*ANNE GILBERT*

## The Owl's Nest    Cloth, net 75c.

"This is the account of a vacation among 'isms.' Followers of some of the fantastic cults and simple Christians met together in a country boarding house and the result is certainly interesting."—*Missions*.

*ISABEL G. and FLORENCE L. BUSH*

## Goose Creek Folks    A Story of the Kentucky Mountains

Illustrated, 12mo, cloth, net $1.00.

A story of real life among the mountaineers of Kentucky. It is a word picture of aspiration, sacrifice and honor. Humor and pathos mingle with purpose and adventure in a vivid tale of "things as they are" in this primitive Southern community.

# FICTION

CAROLINE ABBOT STANLEY      *Author of*
                                *"The Master of the Oaks"*

## The Keeper of the Vineyard

A Tale of the Ozarks. Illustrated, $1.25 net.

This story of a "return to nature," like the author's "Master of the Oaks," pulsates with real life. The scene lies in the Missouri Ozarks, a melting pot wherein those who seek the solace of nature and a living from the soil fuse their lives with the natives of the Hills in the common quest for liberty and education, love and life.

NORMAN HINSDALE PITMAN

## The Lady Elect

A Chinese Romance. Illustrated by Chinese artists. 12mo, cloth, net $1.25.

Some of the best judges of a good story as well as some of the highest authorities on "Things Chinese" pronounce this story a remarkable combination of the rarest and most irresistible type of pure romance and the truest and most realistic delineation of Chinese life. The novelty of the setting and the situations will win the instant approval of the lover of good fiction.

RICHARD S. HOLMES

## Bradford Horton: Man

A Novel. 12mo, cloth, net $1.25.

Dr. Holmes made a distinct place for himself among lovers of good fiction with his earlier stories, "The Victor," and "The Maid of Honor." Competent critics pronounce this new story the author's best. The hero is a man's man who wins instant admiration. Originality of humor, reality of pathos, comedy and heart tragedy are woven into the story.

MARIETTA HOLLEY     (*Josiah Allen's Wife*)

## Samantha on the Woman Question

Illustrated, 12mo, cloth, net $1.00.

For an entire generation Marietta Holley has been entertaining lovers of good humor. "My Opinion and Betsy Bobbitts" and "Samantha at the Centennial" made her name a household word. This last volume is not only timely but with all its facetiousness, keen and telling in its advocacy of "Votes for Women" and Temperance. It equals anything the author has produced.

CHARLES H. LERRIGO

## Doc Williams

A Tale of the Middle West. Illustrated, net $1.25.

"The homely humor of the old doctor and his childlike faith in 'the cure' is so intensely human that he captures the sympathy of the layman at once—a sympathy that becomes the deepest sort of interest."—*Topeka Capital.*

*I. N. McCASH*

## The Horizon of American Missions

12mo, cloth, net $1.00.

Lectures delivered before the College of Missions. Dr. McCash has treated the subject in a broad and masterful way. The book is a distinct and timely contribution to the subject. Some of the topics treated are:—"A Historic Survey of American Missions," "A Regional Survey of Unmet Religious Needs," "Foreign Elements in the Equitation of American Missions," "Cities Related to the Kingdom of God," "Loyal Church Efficiency," "America Democratizing the World."

*MARY CLARK BARNES and DR. LEMUEL C. BARNES*

## The New America

Home Mission Study Course. Illustrated, 12mo, cloth, net 50c. (post. 7c.); paper 30c. (post. 5c.).

This, the regular text-book for the coming year is on the subject of immigration. The eminent authors are fitted for writing on this theme having given much time to studying the problem.

*LAURA GEROULD CRAIG*

## America, God's Melting Pot

Home Mission Study Course. Illustrated, 12mo, paper, net 25c. (postage 4c.).

The subject chosen for study this year, Immigration, covers so wide a field that it was thought best to prepare a supplemental text book from an entirely different standpoint. The author has written a "parable study" which deals more with lessons and agencies than with issues and processes.

*LEILA ALLEN DIMOCK*

## Comrades from Other Lands

Home Mission Junior Text Book. Illustrated, 12mo, paper, net 25c. (postage 4c.).

This book is complementary to the last volume in this course of study, Dr. Henry's SOME IMMIGRANT NEIGHBORS which treated of the lives and occupations of foreigners in our cities. This latter tells what the immigrants are doing in country industries. Teachers of children of from twelve to sixteen will find here material to enlist the sympathies and hold the interest of their scholars.